It. Goes. So. Fast.

Also by Mary Louise Kelly

Anonymous Sources: A Novel

The Bullet: A Novel

It. Goes. So. Fast.

The Year of No Do-Overs

MARY LOUISE KELLY

Henry Holt and Company
New York

Henry Holt and Company
Publishers since 1866
120 Broadway
New York, New York 10271
www.henryholt.com

Henry Holt® and ® are registered trademarks of Macmillan Publishing Group, LLC.

With thanks to the following publications and news outlets, where portions of several chapters originally appeared, in different form: *The Wall Street Journal*, *Newsweek*, Politico, *Washingtonian*, and NPR.

Library of Congress Cataloging-in-Publication Data

Names: Kelly, Mary Louise, author.
Title: It. goes. so. fast. : the year of no do-overs / Mary Louise Kelly.
Description: First edition. | New York : Henry Holt and Company, 2023.
Identifiers: LCCN 2022052766 (print) | LCCN 2022052767 (ebook) |
    ISBN 9781250859853 (hardcover) | ISBN 9781250859860 (ebook)
Subjects: LCSH: Kelly, Mary Louise. | Working mothers—United States—Biography. |
    Women journalists—United States—Biography. | Motherhood—United States. |
    Mothers and sons—United States.
Classification: LCC HQ759.48 K456 2023 (print) | LCC HQ759.48 (ebook) |
    DDC 306.874/3092—dc23/eng/20221212
LC record available at https://lccn.loc.gov/2022052766
LC ebook record available at https://lccn.loc.gov/2022052767

Our books may be purchased in bulk for promotional, educational, or business use. Please contact your local bookseller or the Macmillan Corporate and Premium Sales Department at (800) 221-7945, extension 5442, or by e-mail at MacmillanSpecialMarkets@macmillan.com.

First Edition 2023

Designed by Gabriel Guma

Printed in the United States of America

10 9 8 7 6 5 4 3 2 1

For James and Alexander
My beautiful boys

If you find a book you really want to read but it hasn't been written yet, then you must write it.

—Toni Morrison

You own everything that happened to you. Tell your stories. If people wanted you to write warmly about them, they should've behaved better.

—Anne Lamott

CONTENTS

It. Goes. So. Fast.

INTRODUCTION

————◆————

MY AGENT CALLED, AS AGENTS DO, TO NUDGE.

"Working on anything? Any chapters for me to read?"

"I wish," I sighed. "I'm way too busy. The newsroom remains bonkers. Just relentless. I'm flat out, all day every day."

"Of course you are. But in the evenings, on the weekends . . ."

"I can't."

"What about . . . a short book? Say, just ten chapters."

"No, seriously. Especially now. This year of all years."

"What? 'This year of all . . .' What does that mean?"

"James is about to be a senior. He's about to turn eighteen. This is my last shot. I've missed so much—so many of his games and concerts and science fairs and field trips—because I was working. And I always told myself, *Next year I'll be there.* Well, I'm out of next years. This is it. My last chance to show up. To be present. This is the year of no more do-overs."

A pause.

"That's it," she said. "That's the book. You've got to write it."

Here goes.

❋

THESE DAYS I COUNT THE WEEKS. Before, it was months. Soon it will be days.

I'm counting the time left before my oldest child leaves home. The time left that the four of us will live together, under this roof, intact as a family. The time left—let's just come out and say it—for me to make a different choice.

This child, whose name is James, loves soccer. Always has. There's a photo of him, age one—one!—tiny soccer ball at his feet and huge grin on his face. Barely able to walk and already learning to dribble. Now fast-forward sixteen years. He's a starting striker on his high school varsity team. He lives for these games. This is a boy so catastrophically, irredeemably messy that even his younger brother, also a teenager, gets grossed out by the chaos. This same boy clears a space in the debris to carefully lay out his uniform the night before a game. Cleats, shin guards, cherished jersey, number 7, all washed and arranged at right angles at the foot of his bed. Game time arrives and the whistle blows and James plays his heart out.

At least, this is what I am told. Varsity games tend to happen on weekdays, around four p.m. Want to know what else happens on weekdays at four p.m.? NPR's *All Things Considered* goes on air. Technology makes possible many once impossible things, but our broadcast engineers have yet to figure out how I might anchor a daily national news program from the bleachers. And so I miss his games. Nearly every one of them. James is actually, mostly, okay with this. His dad attends every game he can; the other parents cheer James on; he comes home and gives me the play-by-play at dinner. I am . . . not so okay with this, but I console myself with the knowledge that there will always be another game. That next time

I'll figure out a way to be there, deadlines be damned, screaming myself hoarse on the sidelines.

Except that the years slip by. Ninth grade slides into tenth slides into eleventh. Suddenly, James is a senior. I'm out of next times. There are no more do-overs.

I swear there are a million well-meaning books about the juggle and work-life balance and leaning in and leaning out and how you can have it all just maybe not all at once. Start reading, though, and you'll find they're nearly all aimed at young parents at the beginning of the whole enterprise. Tome after tome of encouragement and advice for new moms drowning in hormones and guilt in their office cubicles, because their phones have lit up with a picture from day care or the nanny, of their kid happily eating his first banana. *And they're missing it and it's only a damn banana but they'll never get that moment back.* Sister, I've been there.

But here is the thing I did not know: the tug is just as strong when your baby is seventeen as when he is seven weeks or seven months. For me, it is in fact stronger. You blink and the finish line is in sight. Young parents, listen to me: It. Goes. So. Fast.

Most of the working mothers I know have made a pact with themselves. When the job and the kids collide, the kids come first. I have pushed back from the anchor chair in Studio 31, NPR's main studio, in the middle of a live broadcast and announced to my cohost and to the startled director, "I've got to go." One cannot get away with this often. But when a text rolls in from the babysitter and it begins, "We're in the emergency room . . . ," you stand up, and you run.

Another moment: Iraq, 2009. I'm in Baghdad, part of the Pentagon press pool covering a visit by the U.S. secretary of defense. We're all suited up in body armor and helmets, and we're being herded toward Black Hawk helicopters that will fly us to the next press conference, when my cell phone rings. It's the school nurse back in Washington. She wants to tell me that my son—the other one, Alexander, then four years old—is sick. Really sick. How fast can I get there? "The day after tomorrow" would have been the accurate response, but the line mercifully went dead before I had to deliver it. I cried myself to sleep that night in Baghdad. Not long after, I quit my job.

I would not have believed it at the time, but these are the easy calls. Your phone delivers a panicked summons; your heart thrums with love for your child; you stand up and you run. I was a journalist before I was a parent. It is in my bones. But while there are many people who can report the news, there is only one person on this planet who can be mother to my children. It has taken me a long time to understand that the hard calls, the ones that may come back to haunt you, are the ones that accumulate in the vast gray space between the drama of a nurse tracking you down in Iraq and . . . the routine Thursday afternoon unfolding of a high school soccer game. I don't stand up and sprint from the studio for the latter because there are so many of them. *Were* so many of them.

I'm aware that I'm lucky to have a choice in how I spend my time. And I don't presume to judge others who've chosen differently, or who seem at peace with their choices. Hats off. (Only could *you* please write the next book and clue the rest of us in on how it's done?) I also know that not everyone reading this is a mother. Not everyone reading this is a parent. This is my story. Yours will be different. What we have in common is the knowledge that there will never be enough hours in the day or enough years on this earth to do everything we came here to do.

This is the last year, ever, that my firstborn is guaranteed to live under the same roof as me. It's also the year I lost my dad, and the year I turned fifty, and the year we all began to emerge from a pandemic that rendered our lives unrecognizable. If all that's not a ripe opportunity for reflection, I don't know what is.

So: This is a book about what happens when the things we love—the things that define and sustain us—come into conflict. It's a book about the unsettling but exhilarating feeling of glimpsing that life as we know it is about to swerve. I have no idea what the transition to an empty nest will look like. As a professional interviewer, I've learned that one of the worst questions you can ask someone is "What's your prediction for what's going to happen in the future?" The only remotely honest answer the poor soul can give is, "Who the hell knows?"

I do know that an interesting exercise is to think of your life as a play. On what scene would you sweep open the curtain? How big is the cast? How many acts would you require? In mine, Act I was my youth. The action here starts slow and builds to school and first love and college and grad school and first job and getting married and buying a car and buying a house and a bunch of other so-called grown-up milestones. That's all Act I.

Why? Because in terms of completely upending your life, all that pales in comparison to having kids. Kids are Act II. You don't get much sleep in Act II. Multiple scenes climax with an exhausted voice offstage muttering, "Because I said so, that's why." The costume budget, at least in our house, is consumed by diapers and then by sports uniforms. But my God, the unscripted moments. The ad-libs of silliness and simple wonder. In Act II, you laugh. A lot.

Act III is the one I'm staring down now. I confess to a quiet fear that it will prove anticlimactic. How to top Acts I and II? When I stalk the stage slower and grayer every year? When surely all the juicy plot twists are behind me? And yet, friends, there's this: The stage at last is ours. The script all ours to write. We do actually, kinda know what we're doing by Act III. Better, we may still have the energy to get up there and do it. Then there's the fact that we don't have much choice about the matter. Act III is the one where it dawns on us that there may not be an infinite number of acts, that we'd best get on with making the most of this one.

Which prompts a delightful, nerve-racking question or two: What now? What next?

CHANGING PLACES

———◦—————

SO MUCH OF LIFE DEPENDS ON WHAT WE CHOOSE TO SEE.
One of my first editors instructed me to play it straight in my reporting. Just the facts. Fine, but which ones? Facts that strike me as essential to a story might strike you as irrelevant. Details that catch my eye might not catch yours. Ask a dozen eyewitnesses to a shooting what they saw, what they heard, how it started. You'll end up with a dozen different, often directly contradictory accounts.

Take the day I was walking along M Street, the main drag of shops and cafés in our Washington, DC, neighborhood, wheeling a stroller and picking applesauce out of my hair. I was on extended, unpaid leave from NPR. At least, that was my plan. NPR was not holding a job for me. There was no guarantee that the national security beat, or any other beat, would be open when I returned. If I returned. My chair and desk, in a coveted corner spot facing a sunny window, had been reassigned to another reporter. I had handed in my microphone and reporter's gear. My press credentials to cover the State Department and Congress were allowed to expire. It was hard to step away. I had been on a roll at work, breaking stories, building a Rolodex of sources, some of whom were finally returning my calls.

But Alexander was two years old and had yet to speak. No baby talk, no cooing, no babbling. At his annual checkup, the young pediatrician filling in for our usual doctor had fixed me with a hard stare.

"Does he say *Mama*?" she asked. "*Dada*? Anything?"

"No. He points to what he wants."

"Does he say *Moo*? *Baa*? Does he blow bubbles?"

I shook my head. We hadn't been overly concerned because we could tell he understood us. We could tell he was smart. Ask him to point to a picture of a bus, a baker, a doggy—and he would nail every one. Why wouldn't he say the words? Beats me. I figured the kid would talk when he was ready.

The pediatrician disagreed.

"It's well outside the normal range," she pronounced. Were we planning on mainstream schooling down the road? If so, Alexander needed intervention, pronto. Why had we waited so long? She sent us home with three urgent to-do items. First, we were to consult an audiologist. Perhaps he couldn't speak because he couldn't hear? Second, we were to learn basic sign language, "so you can communicate with each other." But it was the third one that took my breath away, that had me in tears as I settled the bill and lugged Alexander back to the car. He needed intensive speech therapy, two or three days a week. He would probably need it for a while, she warned. No quick fixes. And success would rest largely on us, the parents—on how invested my husband and I were in the process. Even the best speech therapist could only accomplish so much in an hour, so after each session, homework would follow. Exercises and games to reinforce the lessons. Alexander's rate of progress would depend on how hard we worked with him the other twenty-three hours in a day.

Part of what had me in tears was that my other twenty-three hours a day were already spoken for. There was nothing left after work, sleep, and racing home to see my kids. If I could have outsourced brushing my teeth in those years, I would have.

We had an excellent nanny at that time, organized and energetic. She was great about meals and laundry and planning playdates. But none of the recommendations we received for therapists were within walking distance, and our nanny didn't drive. Also English was her second language. It didn't seem ideal to put someone in charge of helping a kid speak English who was still mastering the language herself. And did I mention that half the time, when our other son was not in nursery school, she had him in tow? James, then four years old and chattering merrily away? Together, the boys were already more than a handful. There was no universe in which it felt right to ask our nanny, on top of everything, to shepherd Alexander through intensive speech therapy.

My husband and I discussed it, but it was a pretty short conversation. Alexander needed us. Neither Nick nor I had the kind of job where we could block off whole mornings several days a week. He traveled regularly for work, often on short notice. I also traveled regularly for work, often on even shorter notice. Breaking news is by definition unpredictable. Meanwhile, Nick made more money than I did. Giving up his paycheck would involve more radical lifestyle changes than giving up mine. So I found myself back in my editor's office, explaining that while, yes, I had indeed only recently returned from my second maternity leave in less than three years, I would now be needing another full year at home. At least.

This is how I came to be pushing a stroller down M Street, applesauce clotted in my hair. I was singing to Alexander. (*Keep talking to him, keep verbalizing, even if he doesn't answer. . . .*) We were nearly at the park, nearly past our reflections in the sidewalk windows of a chic coffee shop, when I spotted a familiar face coming out the door.

"Annie!"

Annie was also a reporter, with another big news organization. (Annie is not her real name; I've changed it to protect her privacy.) Our beats had overlapped. She had scooped me, more than once. She was good. I'd never hung out with her, but I remembered we had been pregnant around the same time, had kidded each other about morning sickness and trying to make it through overly hot, overly long press conferences without barfing. She must have a child around the same age as Alexander.

"Annie. Hey. How are you?"

She cocked her head, as if she was trying to place me.

Suddenly I saw myself through her eyes. I was probably wearing ancient Gap jeans and a stretched-out sweatshirt. It had been many moons since mascara or eyeliner had touched my face. I can't be sure, but if I had to hazard a guess, I had scuffed clogs on my feet and a Ziploc baggie of Cheerios in my hand, and I was belting out the chorus of "The Itsy-Bitsy Spider."

"Mary Louise! Oh my God! I didn't recog—how *are* you?"

We chatted. Annie looked the same as every other time I'd ever seen her: tailored suit, killer heels, in a hurry. No applesauce detectable in her hair. She leaned down and smiled at Alexander.

"Hi there! How are you, little guy?"

Needless to say, no reply.

"I have a daughter around your age," Annie cooed. "Maybe you two can play together sometime?"

Alexander gazed thoughtfully at her. Then he reached for me, straining against the stroller straps and furiously squeezing his fingers into a fist, as though he were yanking a cow's udder. American sign language for "milk." One of the only signs we ever mastered.

Annie straightened back up. "It's soooo good to see you. I'll tell everyone I bumped into you. I have to run. Interview that I've been trying to land for ages, at the White House. Take care!" Her arm shot up and a taxi appeared, and in a flash, she and her stilettos and her gloriously applesauce-free hair were gone.

I would love to report that I carried on with the morning unperturbed, blissfully at peace with my life choices. I did not. I felt like I'd been slapped. Not by Annie but by what she represented, which was everything that I had given up. The places I wanted to go, the prizes I wanted to win. The chance to apply my degrees and my training and my ambition to purposeful work. Work that bore witness, that held powerful people to account. I loved my son, don't get me wrong. The work that he and I were doing was important too, and I knew it could not be outsourced. It wasn't that I regretted my choices. It was that Annie hadn't recognized me. And in that moment, seeing myself through her eyes . . . I didn't recognize myself.

✳

IT WAS A LONG TIME BEFORE I SAW HER AGAIN. Alexander started speaking. It took months, and it came slowly and then all at once. The kid talked when he was ready. I went back to work. My old beat, reporting on the CIA and other spy agencies, had indeed been claimed by another reporter. But there was an opening to cover the Department of Defense. Soon I had a Pentagon hard pass and was trailing the SecDef from NATO headquarters in Belgium to Saudi Arabia to Afghanistan, filing from every stop and from the plane itself.

Annie, meanwhile, had left journalism. She launched a writing consultancy business that allowed her to work from home. I learned this through the journalist grapevine and also a LinkedIn

post or two. She emailed once to ask if I was interested in collab-
orating, perhaps taking on a freelance project? I was nearly too
busy to reply.

When we finally bumped into each other again, outside a wine
bar on Fourteenth Street, it was Annie who spied me first.

"You look great!" she said. "How's the Nat Sec beat? Most days
I don't miss it. But some . . ."

I nodded. Been there.

Then: "You know, I cried all day after that time I bumped into
you."

What? Why?

"Because of how sweet you looked, headed off to the park
together. It was this beautiful morning, and there I was, stressed
out and squeezed into Spanx. Off to interview some senior administration official who refused to be quoted by name and was probably lying through his teeth, while I paid a stranger at day care
to take my baby to the park. I spent the rest of the day thinking,
What the hell am I doing?"

"But I was a mess," I protested.

"You looked happy. Your son looked happy."

"I was terrified I'd thrown away my career."

"You were singing," she said softly.

MY TAKEAWAY FROM THIS ENCOUNTER HAS EVOLVED OVER THE
YEARS.

It is of course the classic tale of how the grass is always greener.
Of how working moms can have it all, just maybe not all at once. I
roll my eyes when people wax on about this, but like most clichés,
there's a big lump of truth in there. Not one of us, not a single
one, has figured out how to be in the park with our kid and be at

a high-power White House meeting at the same time. Perhaps the secret to a happy life isn't about making the right choices so much as learning to live with the ones we do make.

When I decided to write this, I hunted down Alexander's old medical file. I wanted to double-check my memory of events. Stuffed behind the hospital bill for his delivery, amid yellowed insurance statements and immunization records, I find a note, written by me. It's a small piece of paper ripped from our pediatrician's prescription pad; it must have been one of those rare moments when I found myself without a reporter's notebook in hand and had to ask for something, anything, to write on. The note is not dated but it is almost certainly from that day, the day of his two-year checkup. "Speech Language Pathology," I've written, capitalized and framed by quotation marks; the term was not yet familiar.

I notice my handwriting is neater than it is today, a round, looping cursive that bears traces of the way I was taught to write as a girl. I've taken down the names of multiple specialists at Children's National Hospital. Fax numbers (this was 2007) where I'm supposed to submit a diagnosis code. Phone numbers to call for appointments, including one for "Building Blocks Therapy," which I have no memory of visiting, though a later series of receipts suggests we were indeed there, more than once.

Staring at this note, all these years later, I feel my chest tighten and my breathing quicken. I had forgotten how frightened I had been. Frightened that something was seriously wrong, frightened that I had failed my son. I run my fingers over the careful cursive and wonder: Did I really use to write like that? Or was I clutching the pen in a death grip, exerting control over the only thing that I could control, desperately trying to hold it together in that doctor's office? I look at that cursive and I see a mother's fear ferociously channeled into a to-do list of actionable items. Because maybe if I could just identify the right fax number for the right specialist, Alexander would be okay.

✳

ALEXANDER IS FIFTEEN NOW. Taller than me, a varsity athlete. He shaves and lifts weights, and when he asks whether friends can come over on a Friday night, at least half of them are teenage girls. The other day he announced he wanted to run for an elected position at school, one that requires regular public speaking. The campaign itself entailed a speech. Classmates would vote after hearing each candidate address the entire grade, both students and faculty.

We practiced. His speech was good. I told him so. Reminded him to slow down and to make eye contact. That afternoon, he bounced in from school with a smile on his face.

He'd won.

Here's the thing: it had not crossed my mind, not until that moment, what a goddamn miracle that is. The boy who wouldn't speak, delivering a speech. The boy with whom I sat through hour after hour of therapy, coaxing him to say a single word—that same boy, rising to stand before his peers and eloquently explain why they should elect him to represent them. This is Alexander's victory, but I want to crow: Look how far we've come! Look how you've grown! Sweet baby boy, we did it!

Annie swims into my thoughts. I lost touch with her years ago. I wonder where she is, what triumphs she and her own now-teenager might be savoring today. I hope her consulting business has been a raging success, and that her daughter is a stone-cold genius and a really nice kid to boot. I hope Annie still wears fabulous shoes. I hope she has no regrets about leaving journalism.

If I ever bump into her again, I want to say this:

I have thought of you so many times. How we looked at each other and all we could see were our own shortcomings. How we beat ourselves up for failing to accomplish the impossible, for failing to find a way to be in two places at once. When in fact we—and our babies—were doing just fine. When the world could not have cared less whether we showed up in stilettos or in clogs, whether our hair was sleek or sticky with applesauce, whether we were headed to the White House or to a playground. All that was required of me, it turns out, was that I see myself through your eyes. Not as the frumpy has-been that I imagined you saw, but a radiant mother, on a sun-streaked morning, teaching her son to raise his voice in song.

So much of life—*so much*—depends on what we choose to see.

STICKING THE LANDING

———◦———

S OOOOO . . . WALK ME THROUGH YOUR THINKING HERE AGAIN?" My husband, Nick. He's reacting to the announcement I've just made, that I'm writing a book. This book. That I intend to write about this year, as we live it, in real time.

I take a deep breath. "I do recognize the insanity of this."

Nick eyes me coolly. "How do you mean?"

"I mean, I recognize that I already work all the time and that I miss everything. So much of the boys' stuff. And I promised myself that this year would be different. That I would say no more often, and guard every second, and show up, and be present. And instead here I am signing up for what amounts to a second full-time job."

"Signing up to write an entire book on deadline. Due in nine months."

"Yes."

"I was refraining from pointing that out."

Right. He's right. It is indeed insane. The only way I can explain it to him, or even to myself, is that I want this year . . . to stick.

It has to do with the contrast to my day job. Work in daily

STICKING THE LANDING ✦ 17

broadcast news for any length of time and you develop a love-hate relationship with deadlines.

On the plus side, they are marvelous for focusing one's energies. You are forced to be productive. It is not optional. My team and I have to produce a two-hour newsmagazine every day, whether we wake up in the morning brimming with brilliant ideas or not. The pace varies depending on the volume of news and the length of each story, but that's around twenty interviews, features, and enterprise reports a day, every day. You can feel the panic levels rising as the clock ticks toward four p.m., when we go on air. It's not unusual at 4:01 p.m. for almost none of the stories to be filed, edited, and ready. It's not unusual for that to include the lead story, which we need to hit at 4:06 p.m., the second after the national newscast ends.

On some days the news gods smile and all the interview requests come back "yes" and the perfect turn of phrase pops into your head the moment before the on-air light glows green and your mic goes live. You nail it. On other days you want to scream with frustration at how much better you could have made an interview, if you'd just had an extra hour to prep. Actually, scratch that—if you'd just had an extra five minutes to prep. Either way, though, it's done. It's over. The next day's a clean slate. You wake up and the world once again feels full of possibility. You can chase an interview with anyone in the world to discuss any story that sparks your curiosity; how crazy fun is that? I adore this about my job.

But the flip side of every day being a clean slate is that the work can feel ephemeral. You might conduct the most powerful interview, write the most beautiful copy, uncover the most surprising detail, and the next day—*poof.* You have to start all over again. The news cycle marches on. A story that aired a week ago might as well belong to another lifetime.

More than once, I've had editors come to me with a guest they want to book for the show. Sure, I nod, and then I'll start running through the vetting questions: Who are they? What's their agenda? What group do they represent? Any red flags in their background? Are they a good talker? And more than once, the editors have smiled and said—*Well, you should know.* They wave a transcript before me that reveals that not only has the desired guest already been on *All Things Considered*, but that I myself have interviewed them.

There are so many interviews. Each is all-consuming in the moment, but then you're galloping on to the next. Nothing sticks.

I want this year to stick. I want to lay down markers, to be intentional about the way I navigate it. And I want to sit with the decisions I've made that got us here, the trade-offs that to my surprise have gotten harder, not easier, as the boys have grown. I want to record and reckon with my choices while I'm still living them. Both the things that I've gotten wrong—my kids would confidently assure you there's enough material there to fill a book in and of itself—and the things that maybe, somehow, I might get right.

First up: the college visit.

CHICAGO

————◆————

IT IS TWO O'CLOCK ON A GLORIOUS FALL AFTERNOON, AND JAMES AND I ARE TUCKED INTO THE FRONT ROW OF A LECTURE HALL. We're at the University of Chicago, on the main quad, having flown in that morning for an official visit and information session. In the rows behind us sit a few dozen other sets of eager, nervous parents and potential applicants. Up on stage, an admissions officer is running through his sales pitch.

More than fifty UChicago grads have gone on to be Rhodes scholars, he informs us. The college offers a choice of fifty-three majors. Ninety-three Nobel laureates are associated with the university. We learn about undergrad sports, dorms, and the meal plan. Questions?

Hands shoot up.

"How hard is it to do a double major?"

"Do you give credit for AP exams?"

"What percentage of upperclassmen live on campus?"

"What happens if you hate your roommate?" At that last one,

I see James fighting the urge to swivel around and fix the guy with a look of disdain. *Really, dude? That's the best you could come up with?*

"There's a process for that," the admissions officer answers patiently. "You won't be stuck with an awful roommate forever. Next?"

Toward the end of the hour, a group of current undergraduates materializes in the back of the hall. Our walking-tour guides. They dance in a conga line down the center aisle toward the stage then introduce themselves, each sharing their name, preferred pronouns, and favorite juice. Orange and mango are the front-runners, until the last woman to speak.

"Fruit punch," she purrs, followed by a dramatic pause to allow the full subversive weight of this to sink in. Her fellow docents erupt in a chorus of oohs and ahhs.

"That was random," says James, under his breath, and I am reminded once again how much I love this kid.

Outside the lecture hall, we split into smaller groups. I like our guide immediately. She's on Team Mango. She sets a brisk, peppy pace and points out dining halls, where the food is awesome; the main library (the coffee shop inside stays open super late; it's awesome); and the gym where her crew team trains in the winter ("so awesome"). At one point our guide's roommate spots us across the lawn and runs up to say hi. "Welcome!" she smiles. "You guys got the best tour guide on campus! She's awesome!" We learn that the roommate is pre-med, a varsity track star, and student manager of the aforementioned night-owl coffee shop. She seems, objectively, awesome.

The campus is prettier than I'd expected, for such a big university in such a big city. Everything feels clean and very green, tree-shaded paths leading from one massive Gothic façade to the next. Someone with a sense of humor has placed maroon UChicago face masks on the gargoyles guarding one of the main gates, the loops tucked neatly behind their pointy stone ears. The whole place feels well-kept and logically laid out. Numbered cross streets divide it into a grid of right angles. So it takes me a moment to put my finger on why I feel so disoriented.

It's the mental adjustment I'm having to make. James looks so . . . small. My manifestly not-small son—he's six feet one and built like an athlete—looks tiny on this huge campus. I'm so used to seeing him stride the halls of the school he's attended since fifth grade. He fills those halls; he walks like he owns them. Now he's about to revert to very-small-fish-in-very-big-pond status. I remember how little he once looked on the playground of our neighborhood park, when he was a toddler and the "big kids," meaning the six-year-olds, raced past on scooters and threatened to knock him over. How little he looked that first day of a new school for fifth grade, when impossibly tall seniors (I'm talking true giants, some of them standing six feet one) raced past in the stairwell and threatened to knock him over. Here in Chicago, I'm struggling once again to recalibrate. To fathom how a baby whose whole world was once the playpen in the corner of my kitchen is now happily exploring a university of thousands, in a city of millions.

Watching my son wander this campus sweeps me with a mixture of pride and vertigo. It's like the day, cleaning out a closet, that I stumbled across his very first pair of shoes and held them up beside the stinky men's size 11 sneakers he'd just kicked off by the front door. How was he ever so small? How has he possibly grown so big? James seems to feel it too. "It's going to be weird," he says, "to be the youngest again."

IN SCOTLAND, WHERE MY HUSBAND WAS BORN AND RAISED, COL-LEGE VISITS ARE NOT A THING.

"I don't get it," says Nick. "Doesn't he just apply to a bunch of places, and the best school he gets in, he goes there? Why does he actually need to see the place?"

Fair point. But Nick's framing fails to consider American notions about life, liberty, . . . and the pursuit of happiness. I'm pretty sure any of the schools on James's short list have the academic resources to keep him busy. But what about happy? If things go to plan, James is picking where he'll spend the next four years of his life. It would be nice if, you know, he liked the place. And I don't know how he could tell from the glossy brochures that flood our mailbox these days, or from a virtual info session on Zoom. Doesn't any institution look great when it's completely in control of what you see?

What strikes James on this visit is interesting. As we walk, he keeps up a running commentary. He's curious about dorm life. He listened closely to the spiel about the rich variety of student activities and clubs. But the statistic he's already memorized from today's talk is this one: *an acceptance rate of 83–93 percent for UChicago students at top 15 law schools.*

"That's really impressive, isn't it?" he asks.

Yes, I agree. It sure is.

"Should we walk over and look at the law school later?"

We do. It's impressive too. It's only later that I get to thinking: *Good Lord, these poor kids.* James and zillions of high school seniors like him, not even in college yet and already steeling themselves for grad school applications. It's such a treadmill. I want to whisper: *Just enjoy this moment. This one, the one happening right now! Stop thinking about the next step, and the one after that.*

I am admittedly lousy at heeding this advice myself. I am ambitious, always have been, and there is a relentless quality to ambition. George Saunders captures it beautifully in his book *Congratulations, By the Way.* "You do well in high-school," he writes, "in the hopes of getting into a good college, so you can do well in the good college, in the hopes of a getting a good job, so you can do well in the good job, so you can . . ."

You see where this is going.

"Still," Saunders continues, "accomplishment is unreliable. 'Succeeding,' whatever that might mean to you, is hard, and the need to do so constantly renews itself (success is like a mountain that keeps growing ahead of you as you hike it), and there's the very real danger that 'succeeding' will take up your whole life, while the big questions go untended."

Amen.

I've starred and underscored every line of that passage in my copy of the book. But it is one thing to read these words and recognize their truth, and quite another to choose to hop off the treadmill in mid-sprint. I'm not sure that even Saunders is totally practicing what he preaches. His book went on to become a *New York Times* bestseller. His online bio notes that over the course of his career, Saunders has won the Man Booker Prize, landed MacArthur and Guggenheim Fellowships, and appeared on *The Colbert Report, Late Night with David Letterman*, and—wait for it—*All Things Considered*. Saunders was named one of the world's one hundred most influential people by *Time* magazine. He has not, in other words, exactly pulled the plug on succeeding.

Personally, it's taken me a while to see that the reward for good work is not that you get to be done. It's that people notice and ask you to do more of it. The mountain keeps growing ahead of you as you hike it.

In my line of work, here's what that looks like: produce good journalism and the interviews you land grow higher in profile. You command more time on air. The invitations to speak get more prestigious. The stakes get higher. And then somebody wants you to come talk about your reporting on their podcast or their cable TV show. They want you to address their class of aspiring journalists, or publish an Op-Ed, or—ahem—write a book. And you want to do all these things, because they are exciting. Because you are building your reputation. Because you want to help the people who have helped you, and you also want to pay it forward, to be a good role model for the young journalists coming up behind you. But the more you say yes . . . the more you show up and meet your deadlines and deliver excellent work . . . the more invitations flood in. The stakes grow higher still. It never stops.

On the one hand, of course, this is the point. Work hard and reap the rewards. But I've noticed a swimming pool quality to my newsroom and, I suspect, to most workplaces. You can be the most talented, industrious employee in the joint. The colleague who works around the clock, the guy in constant demand, the one they can't function without. But if you *do* leave? The water closes up over you. The show must go on. Others will slot in and assume your responsibilities. The ripples overhead grow smaller and then smaller still, and in no time it's as if you never were.

I find myself questioning the point of all this when it comes to my kids, in ways that I don't—or at least haven't yet—when it comes to myself. Yes, of course, I want my child to succeed. Yes, I want him to dream big and charge headfirst at life and shake whatever he wants from it. But my most fervent mother's wish is just . . . that he be happy. That he find real friends, and a partner who is good to him and makes him laugh. That he live his life in a way that leaves others around him a little happier too. In the end, what else is there? What otherwise *is* the point of it all?

It's a long walk from the law school back to our hotel, forty minutes or so. James and I stroll side by side, each lost in our thoughts. I wonder if today has left him stressed about his college applications, all those essays he still has to write. Or perhaps he's moved on to contemplating the LSAT? As for me, I'm thinking about the guy who asked about hating your roommates. Maybe it wasn't such a dumb question after all; life is too short to bunk with jerks. But one of the joys of college is learning to live with and appreciate people who see the world in radically different ways than you do, who grew up in radically different homes, with different values. As we walk, I start to smile. I'm imagining the full cast of characters James will have to learn to live with, the adventures he will have, the stories he will tell us, when he comes back home.

IT EMERGES THAT, NO, JAMES WAS NOT CONTEMPLATING THE LSAT. He was contemplating his social plans for the evening.

"Mom, would you mind if I leave dinner a little early?" he asks.

I have booked a nice restaurant for tonight. A table for two, near campus on Chicago's South Side, at a place that serves Southern soul food. (I'll confess to being a smidge skeptical about this, having grown up in Georgia, where we know our way around soul food.) I had been looking forward to more one-on-one time with my oldest, relishing the idea of getting him to myself. It rarely happens at home in DC. The rest of the family is usually kicking around, and James moves in a pack of friends on the weekends. But here in Chicago, am I not the only person he knows?

As we settle into a window table and a plate of biscuits and spicy pimento cheese (delicious, fine, I admit it), James's phone keeps lighting up. A few high school acquaintances are now enrolled here at the university; does James want to hang out? Social media has revealed that a friend from summer camp two years ago is here too, not to mention several former teammates from his travel soccer team. James has gone from knowing no one in this town, to fielding multiple invitations to BBQs and parties this weekend. At least one of these parties would appear to be starting right now.

By the time our main course appears—gumbo thick with

chicken, andouille sausage, and Carolina Gold rice—James is antsy, stealing glances at his phone. He is briefly distracted by the arrival of a cast-iron skillet of cornbread (which, with apologies to the formidable cooks of Georgia, is the best I've ever tasted). But it's clear he's itching to find a ride and be on his way. I have to laugh. This is the way it's supposed to work. You raise them, and then you let them go. Also, chalk one up for George Saunders. My son appears to have many things on his mind tonight, not one of which involves "succeeding" at anything beyond having a great time. Halfway through my gumbo, I release James into the night. He's gone like a shot.

I'm on the last sip of my cocktail and trying to catch our waiter's eye for the check when James reappears.

"Mom. Will you be okay getting back to the hotel yourself?"

"You came back to check?"

He nods.

Two thoughts pop into my head in quick succession. The first is that I just completed my latest round of hostile environment training, which NPR requires before we travel on riskier assignments. They teach us how to apply tourniquets, how to stanch catastrophic bleeding from gunshot or land mine wounds, and, if necessary, how to escape terrorists by rappelling out of hotel windows. Seriously, this is covered on the course. My job has required me to file from a runway under mortar fire in Afghanistan, from the deck of an aircraft carrier deployed in wartime to the Adriatic Sea, and from Tehran, from the middle of a vast crowd of people with their fists in the air, shouting, "Death to America." So yes, kiddo, I think I can manage walking the two blocks to our hotel, on the still early side of a nice evening in Chicago. I bite my tongue and refrain from saying any of this.

The second thought is wonder.

What James has just asked is such a simple question, but it's one that I can say with confidence he would not have thought to ask a year or two ago. My boy is becoming a man; my child is becoming an adult, an empathetic human beginning to shoulder the weight of caring for others. I think of the countless carpools I've sorted for him, the countless hours devoted to worrying about how he or his brother are going to get home safely from somewhere. The nights waiting up, to be sure they make curfew. And now, for the first time, the roles reverse.

My heart feels suddenly huge, swollen with love. Swollen, too, with something like sadness. I am fiercely proud of the young man before me. I also fiercely miss the boy he was. A little boy who would not have thought to worry about his mother, because he thought she was invincible; he thought the sun and moon revolved around her and that she ruled the world.

"Mom?"

"I'll be fine, sweet boy. Thanks for checking."

"Okay. Love you."

"Have fun."

He kisses the top of my head. Turns. And then, for good this time, he's gone.

KEEPING WATCH

————◦►◦————

MY EYES SNAP OPEN AT THREE A.M., AND WHAT I AM THINKING ABOUT IS THE DOG.

Thunder has woken me, banging and booming overhead. Lightning is splitting the night sky, again and again and again. The heaviest rain I've ever heard in this house is slamming against the windows, slamming so hard I fear the panes will shatter. I check my phone in the dark. A tornado watch and flood warning are in effect until dawn. These are the remnants of a Category 4 hurricane, blown up from the Gulf, and if these are the remnants, I can't imagine what it was like to witness the real deal.

Our dog, like a lot of dogs, does not like thunderstorms. I, meanwhile, do not like dogs. You might not either, if they made your throat close tight and your eyes go scratchy and your chest and arms puff up in lumpy pink hives. Shadow, our Bernedoodle, is allegedly hypoallergenic. Shaggy and smelly and an enthusiastic backyard digger, prone to wandering around the kitchen with mud clumps and twigs clinging to his snout—but hypoallergenic. When he falls asleep on top of my bare feet at dinner, usually the worst that happens is I have a sneezing fit. Shadow is ferocious in his pursuit of squirrels and the UPS guy. He cowers in the face of bumblebees, fireworks, . . . and thunder. He must be petrified.

I rise from bed and pad downstairs in my nightgown, to find Alexander and Shadow huddled in the dark, in the hall outside the boys' bedrooms. I say "dark" because the lights are switched off, but the lightning is coming nonstop now, illuminating the scene like a gaudy neon motel sign cycling on and off. Alexander looks sleep glazed, slumped against the wall. Shadow is swaying, visibly trembling with terror. I reach down and touch his furry belly. His heart is racing.

"He won't sleep," says Alexander, voice weary and eyes drooping. "He won't climb into bed. He's been like this for an hour. Just whimpering. I don't know what to do." My teenage son is nearly whimpering himself.

Shadow is Alexander's dog. I never wanted a dog. Did I mention I don't like dogs?

But on June 4, 2015—it's neatly dated at the top—Alexander had written us a letter.

"Dear Mom and Dad," it begins. "When you read this note I hope you are happy and have a smile on your face. The reason I am writing this note is because I want a dog."

What follows is an onslaught of charm, cunning, and righteousness that defense attorneys would do well to study before putting a client on the stand.

"I have a few reasons why I want a dog," continues Alexander, then age nine. "When I am sad, it could comfort me." That's reason number two. (Reason number one: "It would be a good friend to me.") In thick pencil, on lined school notebook paper, Alexander builds to what he must have sensed would be the devastating deal closer: "My last reason is that I could get off my iPad and play with the dog. I would not use my iPad a lot!"

He begged for two years before we caved. This letter was just the closing salvo. Starting at age seven, whenever anyone asked what he wanted for his birthday or for Christmas, Alexander would lower his head in sorrow before staring sweetly into his questioner's eyes. "Nothing. Because the one thing in the world that I really want, which is a dog, I'm not allowed to get. My mom and dad won't let me. Do you know what that's like? To know that there's only one thing in the whole world that will make you happy and that you will never, ever get it? Anyway, what do *you* want for Christmas?"

Nick is not a dog person either. Neither of us pleaded for a puppy when we were kids. I had lobbied hard for a pony, turned out to be allergic to them too, and settled for a scrawny pair of chameleons named King Arthur and Lancelot who lived in a terrarium in the basement, eventually escaped, and went on to reproduce wildly in our back yard. Nick's best effort in the childhood pet department was a green-and-gold parakeet named Spike, whose party trick was kicking a walnut-sized soccer ball across the kitchen floor. After we grew up and got married and had kids, we were united in our lack of enthusiasm for acquiring a family dog. The last thing we needed was another living creature in our care that required feeding, bathing, and regular toenail trims. James never asked for a dog. When Alexander did, repeatedly, we tried to distract him with Legos and ice cream and hikes in the woods. We figured it was a phase, and like all phases, it would pass.

No joy. Alexander was relentless. That June 2015 letter ends: "P.S. I will definitely take care of it!" By the end of the summer, I was online and googling breeders. That fall, Shadow arrived. I am forced to concede that Alexander has been true to his word. He walks the dog every day. He administers the monthly flea and tick pills, disguising the medicinal taste inside lumps of sharp

Cheddar cheese. On weekends, when we're all running in opposite directions, he's the one pinging the family group text, making sure someone remembers to fill the dog's water dish. But tonight, looking at my son slumping against the wall and Shadow quivering in the lightning-shot hallway, I can tell he's hit his limit.

"Come here," I command, and lead them into Alexander's bedroom. My son flops against the pillows. Even with the blinds closed, the lightning is intense. Wind rattles the windows in their frames. Shadow paces, whining and rigid with tension. It takes a long time to drag him onto the bed and then settle him across my lap. Eventually we manage, and I sit with one hand on the head of the dog, the other on the head of my son.

When the boys were small, when they shared a room and allowed me to tuck them in and tell them stories, we had a ritual. Every night I would attempt to regale them with adventures of furry woodland animals, like the Reddy Fox stories that I had cherished as a girl. And every night they would howl in protest and demand Batman, ideally in cahoots with the Hulk, and if the bad guy perished in a plot twist involving burping or flatulence, so much the better. It was only when their eyes at last grew heavy that my favorite part of bedtime came. In the darkness, perched on the edge of the bed, I would stroke their tangled hair and tell them how much I loved them. How they were the smartest, strongest, fastest, funniest, kindest boys in all the land. "So clever," I would whisper. "So sweet. So silly. So brave. So loved."

Under the covers, their feet would twitch and their breathing would slow. "I'll always take care of you. Always protect you, always look out for you. Always love you." The house would exhale and go quiet.

It had been years. I'd almost forgotten the words, the rhythm of them. These days I go to bed before my children. They're up doing homework or texting friends until the wee hours, and I'm the one struggling to keep my eyes open past ten p.m. So many, many nights had passed since anyone had demanded a bedtime story. But sitting there with my hand on the dog, out of nowhere, the instinct returned. "You're the best dog in the whole world," I told him. "So sweet. So silly. So brave."

We stayed that way a long time. Shadow shaking, rain beating down, thunder pounding. Words pouring out of me.

Always take care of you. Always protect you, always look out for you. The best dog in all the land.

My thoughts flew back to another night, another storm, another house. When James was born, we were living three blocks away. It was a smaller house, painted white with black shutters, with a narrow guest room at the back that became his nursery. I remember feeding him there, rocking him in a new glider chair of which I was immensely proud, as ominous blue-black clouds rolled in. James must have been a few weeks old.

For days, weather forecasters had been warning that the storm of the decade was on its way. It was the first time I felt the spine-stiffening adrenaline of being a Responsible New Parent. I was the thing standing between this tiny, defenseless human and the wild world about to rage outside our house. As a Responsible New Parent, I had actually heeded the news-you-can-use, pre-storm advice that I would have ignored when it was just Nick and me. In the kitchen, I'd piled crates of bottled water and canned soup. In the basement, stocks of flashlights and batteries, candles and matches. I had no idea yet what I was doing as a mother, but I knew how to fill a shopping cart at Target.

Wedged into the glider with James, the sky darkening above us, I thought of a play that had been assigned in college. Shakespeare, the famous scene from *King Lear*, where Lear calls on a storm to do its worst:

Blow, winds, and crack your cheeks! Rage, blow!
You cataracts and hurricanoes, spout
Till you have drench'd our steeples, [drown'd] the cocks!

I couldn't summon the exact quote in the moment. We had a Shakespeare anthology kicking around somewhere in the house, but I didn't want to wake the baby to stand up and hunt for it. Instead I tucked James's blanket more tightly around his toes and murmured something inspired by *Lear* but considerably less poetic, probably closer to *"Hey, Storm? Bring it."*

The storm did. It ripped the black shutters off our house and tossed them onto the yard below. The basement flooded. My carefully stacked candles and flashlights floated off the shelves. No one ever ate the tinned soup. But that little boy tucked in my arms . . . I kept him safe.

YEARS VANISH AND HERE I AM, IN ANOTHER HOUSE, HOLDING Shadow. His heart is thumping less frantically, slowly returning to normal. I wait to feel his paws twitch with sleep instead of fear. Alexander has nodded off long ago. Or so I thought, until he rolls over and opens one eye.

"Mom, you can go."

"Let me just make sure he's asleep."

"It's fine, Mom. Go back to bed."

For the briefest of moments, I feel stung. Dismissed.

But Alexander is only stating a fact: He needed me, but now he doesn't. He's fine. Shadow is fine. They've got this.

I can't think of another relationship in one's life where you actively root for the other person to outgrow you. Where the whole goal is for them to surpass you, to separate. That's the fundamental tension of parent and child. You can't wait for them to stop being so needy every second, and then they stop needing you every second, and it feels like a stake to the heart.

One night your kids are begging you to tell a Batman and Hulk story and the next they're not. They would rather read *Harry Potter* on their own, thanks very much, and would you please shut the bedroom door on your way out? One night goes by and then two, three, four. Years later, looking back, you will try to pinpoint when it was, the last night. The last time they wanted a story. Because of course you don't know in the moment. When did they stop asking? When did they grow too big? How has it now been so long that you've forgotten the words you used to whisper? So long that it took a reflex, the muscle memory of holding another helpless creature close, to tug the words from deep inside?

One day very soon now, my boys will be men. One day they may keep watch over a child of their own. They will lean close and smooth tangled hair and murmur words of comfort, and when they do, I like to think I'll be there too. That the words I spoke to them when they were children have settled in their bones, are part of them, to be called forth when needed. Just as my mother's voice sometimes mysteriously rises forth from within me.

I was born in Germany, and when I was a little girl, she used to call me her *kaninchen*. German for "rabbit." A term of endearment. "How is my little *kaninchen*?" she would ask. "Hungry for lunch yet?" I'd forgotten this until I was bundling my own child into a winter coat and mittens one day and, without thinking, called him my *kaninchen*. A word that had not crossed my lips in thirty years, that I had never seen written down, that I couldn't have told you how to spell.

My mouth opens but it is my mother who is speaking. The generations keep watch over each other.

✻

IT'S ONLY WHEN I AM BACK UPSTAIRS IN MY OWN BED THAT I REALIZE I NEVER CHECKED ON MY OTHER CHILD. It never occurred to me. James hadn't stirred, hadn't made a peep all night. He has always been a champion sleeper. But might maternal love also play a role in his ability to snore through an unholy racket? Might he have acquired the ability to sleep soundly through a tempest because he's been told his whole life that he is safe?

Always protect you. Always look out for you. Always love you.

You want to keep them under this roof, within these four walls, just one more night. You want it not to be the last. The instinct to keep watch is so strong. I'll blink and James and his brother will be out in the world; life will be hurling cataracts and hurricanoes at them that exceed my powers of protection. This is how it's supposed to work. This is how it has to be. They're fine. They've got this. They needed me, and now—much of the time—they don't.

If you stop to dwell on the people who once needed you and no longer do, the sadness can nearly knock you down. But life is both more complicated and more beautiful than this. I'm fifty years old and still need my mom all the time. On days when I'm struggling, I channel my mother and her confidence in me. On days when I'm really struggling, I picture my grandmothers too, and their mothers before them. A long line of women, many of whom I've never met, whose voices somehow resonate in mine. They must feel as bone-tired as I do. All these thousands upon thousands of nights between us, sitting up in the dark, keeping watch, shushing children and silly dogs to sleep.

When we get it right—when we whisper the incantations just so—the house exhales. Goes quiet. And says good night.

THE HELICOPTER

I SUSPECT THAT FOR EVERY WOMAN WHO'S EVER TRIED TO BALANCE
WORK AND FAMILY, THERE COMES A DAY WHEN YOU HIT THE WALL.
I don't mean your run-of-the-mill bad day, when the baby barfs
down the back of your dress as you're racing out the door. I'm not
even talking about the panic-attack-inducing, babysitter-calls-in-
sick-on-the-morning-of-a-crucial-interview kind of day.

I'm talking about The. Day. You. Hit. The. Wall.

This chapter is the story of the day when I hit mine. I was in
Baghdad, covering a visit by the U.S. secretary of defense. This was
part of my duties on the Pentagon beat, the assignment I accepted
following the year at home with Alexander and the speech therapists. When the defense secretary travels, a press pool hops on the
plane to accompany him. (So far, it's always been a him. So many
bridges yet to cross.) You file on where he goes, who he's meeting,
what arms deals are discussed, what promises the United States is
making to its allies and its adversaries abroad. Sometimes you hur-
tle through two or three countries in a single day. We were often in
war zones. I took nothing like the risks my colleagues based in such

places take; traveling overseas with the defense secretary means traveling in a security bubble. Still, it's safe to assume that any job that requires you to pack bulletproof body armor is not exactly family friendly.

This particular trip had started in Jerusalem. Then it was on to meetings in Amman, followed by a stop at a military airbase near Nasiriya, in the scorched desert of southern Iraq. By the time we arrived in Baghdad, a sandstorm was blowing in. The city was too dangerous for our convoy to risk driving through, so a swarm of Black Hawk helicopters was organized to whisk us all from the airstrip to a press conference at the Iraqi defense ministry.

We were about to board and strap in for takeoff when my phone vibrated. I fumbled for it under my flak jacket and pushed back my helmet to answer.

"Hello, Mrs. Kelly?" came a voice.

It's not easy to hear over the roar of half a dozen helicopters, and I had to ask her to shout. It took a moment to grasp that the caller was the nurse at my children's school, back home in Washington, DC. Apparently my son was sick.

"I need to ask you to come get him," the nurse was yelling.

"Oh, no," I yelled back, my voice catching. "I can't right now. You see, I'm in—"

"No, I don't mean to bring him home," she cut in. "He's really sick. Alexander's having trouble breathing."

"Okay, I . . ." My mind raced. He was four then. Alexander had looked healthy as a horse when I left home three days earlier. But he'd been hospitalized twice before with respiratory infections. He was born early, and very sick.

"I think we need to get him to a doctor," the nurse shouted. "Or to the hospital, even."

I was trying to answer her when the line went dead. The Black Hawk lifted off. My son needed me, again, and I was in a helicopter halfway around the world, gazing down over the snarled traffic of Baghdad.

Just like that, I hit the wall.

✳

THERE WILL BE THOSE WHO READ THIS AND JUDGE. Who will shake their heads and say that mothers of young children have no business jetting off to war zones. Believe me, you wouldn't be saying anything I didn't tell myself that night.

In my defense, I could point out how much I loved my job. Or I could point out how many fathers of young children were on that trip. In fairness, most of them didn't wear their guilt at being away any more lightly than the women did. The press section of every military plane I've ever been on has been filled with men passing around pictures of their kids. Still, one can't help but notice that school nurses rarely call them first. Sometimes the problem isn't the demands of our bosses but the expectations of our society. As one friend—a high-powered editor herself—put it, "Mothers remain the default for everything."

That night in Baghdad, I crawled into the bunk bed where I'd been assigned to sleep, in a trailer parked behind one of Saddam Hussein's abandoned palaces, and I cried. It seemed blindingly obvious that it was time for Plan B. My husband had been telling me for ages that I was armed with better dinner party stories than anyone he knew. Who else had a job that got them invited to the CIA holiday party, or to take tea with Pakistan's prime minister? On the flight home from Iraq to what was then known as Andrews Air Force Base, I started writing a spy novel. I named my protagonist Alexandra James, after my sons, Alexander and James, to remind myself why I was doing it.

Seven months after Baghdad, I resigned from my job at NPR.

No leave of absence this time, no hedging my bets. I flat out quit. It goes without saying that many people wouldn't or couldn't make the decision I did. I might have reacted differently myself at an earlier or later stage in my career. Knowing that I was fortunate to have a choice, when the majority of working parents do not, still didn't make it easy to walk away from a career in which I'd then invested more than fifteen years. But the brutal truth was, I'd had it.

For a while after I left NPR, my typical work schedule looked like this: drop kids at school, write for a few hours, pick up kids, supervise homework and dinner, tuck kids into bed, write for another hour. On a wild day I might have squeezed in a grocery run and a couple loads of laundry too. The life of a jet-setting correspondent it was not.

And yet—with sincere and enormous respect for the accomplishments of my colleagues who were still firmly on the treadmill—I found myself wondering if there wasn't room for a more expansive definition of female professional success. So many women I knew were blending work and family in ways our mothers and grandmothers never dreamed possible. This seemed to me worth celebrating, not sniffing at. Dare I confess that I felt I was accomplishing something just as meaningful in those years writing novels at home, as when I spent my time scurrying between Pentagon press briefings? I started asking my friends in the business world, "Why do we automatically assume the woman running the company is doing more with her life than the woman who has negotiated a three-day week?"

I didn't have a fully formed answer to that. The first time I tried to write about the helicopter incident, in an essay for *Newsweek*, I couldn't even figure out how to end the piece. It felt like I should have some pearl of wisdom to offer, some dramatic zinger of a parting thought. Who was I to write about this stuff, when I was still wrestling with it every day myself?

In the end, fittingly, it was Alexander who rescued me. Three years had passed since Baghdad; my son was now seven years old and robustly healthy. He walked into my study as I sat glaring at my laptop and asked what I was working on.

"Well," I began, "it's an article about trying to be a good mom and be good at your job at the same time."

He nodded solemnly. "You'd be the perfect person to write that, Mom," he said, and then he wandered off to play with Legos.

That was enough to push me over the wall, and then some.

IF YOU'VE MADE IT THIS FAR, YOU'VE FIGURED OUT I DIDN'T STAY AWAY FROM THE NEWSROOM FOREVER. I did write that novel about Alexandra James, had a hoot doing it, and published it in 2013. It did okay. My next one published in 2015 and did better than okay, especially overseas.

The problem with being a full-time novelist, though, was that I never stopped missing the newsroom. The day of my very first big book talk—June 23, 2013—happened to be the same day that ex–National Security Agency contractor Edward Snowden fled Hong Kong, where he'd been hiding, and boarded an Aeroflot flight to Moscow. Snowden had outed himself as the source who had leaked top-secret documents to reporters, detailing clandestine government surveillance programs. The U.S. government had just charged him with espionage. On the one hand, these are fantastic developments if you're trying to hawk a spy thriller titled *Anonymous Sources*. On the other, I was too riveted to concentrate. Would Snowden hop yet another flight to Ecuador? Would he be arrested? Would he end up in passport control/asylum limbo in Moscow's Sheremetyevo airport? I kept sneaking away from my book signing to hide in the bathroom and scroll the latest on Twitter.

Fast-forward two years. November 2015. The Paris terror attacks were the straw that broke this camel's back. News of suicide bombers, of coordinated terrorist attacks in neighborhoods that I had walked and loved, prompted a normal human reaction of horror. They also prompted a reaction unique to journalists and first responders: *I need to go. I need to get on the first plane there.* I speak French, I know Paris well, I had reported on terrorism for years. I'd already traveled to mosques in Hamburg to glimpse where some of the 9/11 hijackers were radicalized. Also to Brussels to investigate efforts to stand up a pan-European counterterrorism unit. What light might the Paris attacks shed on how those efforts were working out? I was desperate to go, desperate to interview everyone in sight and help tell the story. I called every news manager I still knew at NPR and said, in a nutshell, "Put me in, coach."

I started back at NPR as a national security correspondent on January 11, 2016. James by then was twelve years old; Alexander was ten. They were both strong athletes, doing fine in school. It seemed like an okay moment to lean in again. Many times, that first year back, the elevator doors would slide open onto the third-floor newsroom, and I would catch my breath, I was so happy to be there. There is nowhere on earth where I feel as alive as a newsroom erupting in pandemonium, when a big story is breaking. It was such a visceral relief to come home.

I was under no illusion that the juggle would suddenly become easy. The boys might have been older, but there were still only twenty-four hours in a day. Also, minor detail: the year I went back marked the beginning of the Trump news cyclone. The news never stopped; one cycle of outrage, investigation, and fact-checking blurred into the next. The allegations of Russian interference in the 2016 election and the subsequent Mueller inquiry alone were enough to guarantee I rarely slept. "I'm so sorry, I'm going to be late again" became the regular opening line of my texts home to the babysitter. Then came a presidential impeachment, a disputed election, another impeachment, an insurrection. And, oh yeah, a deadly pandemic. There have been days—many days—when I, like every other journalist in Washington, was hanging on by my toenails.

But do you know what would have made me even crazier? If I'd missed it. If I hadn't found a path back into the newsroom. If I'd been stuck watching it all from the sidelines, begging, "Coach, pleeease, put me in put me in put me in." I loved writing fiction. Still do. I plan to write more. But let's be honest: it's tough to make up plot twists wilder than the ones we've all been living through.

✳

IF YOU HAVE HEARD ME CONDUCT A LIVE INTERVIEW ON NPR, CHANCES ARE YOU'VE HEARD ME SAY, "IN THE TIME WE HAVE LEFT . . ." This is because I have no wiggle room. Zip. The show is timed to the precise second. Five times every hour, I have to "hit the post" so that hundreds of NPR stations nationwide can break away to local news and weather, then rejoin the national broadcast at the top of the next segment. So it helps when I'm interviewing, say, a member of the Senate finance committee, to say, "In the minute we have left . . ." or "Just a few seconds left, Senator . . ." I'm signaling to my live guest that this might not be the best time to launch into her brilliant seventeen-point deficit reduction plan. More important, I'm signaling to people listening that I'm not being rude if I have to cut off the guest moments later. Everyone was given fair warning: I need to land this plane.

On the occasions I fail to do this, you'd be amazed how many irate listeners will take to email and Twitter. "Come on, you really couldn't have given the senator another ten measly seconds to finish her sentence?"

No, sir, I really couldn't. Sorry, but it doesn't work that way.

Needless to say, it doesn't work that way in life either. That same phrase—*in the time we have left*—also speaks acutely to this stage of raising children. Of consciously marking the moments, trying to hoard and savor the days, instead of racing through them. I find myself again at an inflection point. There are, despite my best efforts, still only twenty-four hours in a day. And I find that how I want to spend them is shifting. Journalist and author Elsa Walsh nailed this feeling in a 2013 *Washington Post* piece on feminism, work, and what women want, headlined "Why Women Should Embrace a 'Good Enough' Life." Walsh described how her priorities have changed as she's gotten older. And how they change as our children get older too, as we face their imminent departure, rather than worrying about their bedtime. "With my daughter poised to leave for college, all I want is to have more time with her, not less," she writes.

Bingo.

Walsh, whom I didn't know at the time she wrote the essay but who has since become a neighbor and a friend, is no stranger to ambition. She's a former *Post* reporter and *New Yorker* staff writer, a finalist for the Pulitzer Prize. But she is scathing in describing what traditional "success" requires: ever more time at the office, ever more travel, always being available, always a click away.

"Imagine what that life looks like to a child," Walsh demands. "Imagine what it looks like to yourself when you are 80."

That's an intriguing frame through which to view the myriad trade-offs that working parents make. Which ones would I struggle to explain to a child? Which ones will cause my eighty-year-old self to flinch?

I have rarely regretted the times when work and family collided and I chose family. But rarely is not never, and there are moments that haunt me. In 2017, at the height of the Russia story, with new allegations popping every day about Trump and Russia and whether Putin's spy services had dirt—*kompromat*—on the president of the United States, I made a long-shot interview request. Might the director of the SVR, successor to the KGB and Russia's answer to the CIA, take my questions?

Weeks passed in silence and then to my astonishment, an answer came back: yes. My producer and I scrambled to secure visas and plane tickets. Our Moscow bureau scrambled to help with an interpreter and logistics for the interview, which we presumed would take place at the SVR's Yasenevo headquarters, in the suburbs of Moscow. I say "presumed" because we never got that far. With just days to go, the SVR called to say they needed to change the date. They named a new one—a date squarely in the middle of my family vacation—and they refused to budge. I should mention this was a long-planned holiday, with complicated logistics of its own, that would have been impossible to join halfway through. I agonized and agonized and then, with a heavy heart, pulled the plug on the interview. The SVR almost never talks to Western journalists, and despite my repeated requests, they've never said yes again. It was, for the record, a spectacular family trip. And yes, for the record, my eighty-year-old self will bang her head on the table in frustration every time she thinks of it.

It's harder to pinpoint times that went the other way, when I put work over family and regretted it. I can't actually think of a crucial birthday or camp drop-off that I've missed, an absence that I'd be embarrassed to explain to a kid. Alexander has no memory of the time he was so sick that a school nurse tracked me down in Baghdad. He knows that I came home as quickly as I could; he knows his dad was there within the hour.

What I think will give future-octogenarian me pause is not the big decisions but the accretion of all the many, many small ones, none of them seemingly significant in the moment. All those weekday soccer games when I showed up late, or failed to make it altogether. The playdates I skipped, the pool parties that I missed. The school pickups, the chance to hear all the chatter from the back seat. The mornings baking cookies, when it was the nanny in the kitchen instead of me.

It stings to admit that the main (the only?) person bothered by these absences is me. I was the one who failed to grasp quite how abruptly those baking mornings would end, how quickly the boys in footie pajamas would grow into young men with a thousand better things to do than hang with Mom and her rolling pin in the kitchen. The boys were happy so long as there were warm cookies; I can't recall them complaining that they wished I'd been the one to bake them.

To check my memory, I corner James in the hall one day.

"Can you think of a time when you needed me and I didn't come, because I was working?"

He gives me a searching look, then stares at the floor for so long that I'm convinced he's about to really let me have it.

At last he looks up.

"I'm sure there have been, but I can't think of any. Also can I have fifteen bucks for Chipotle?"

I'm about to remind him there's food in the fridge, and that if he wants Chipotle, he has an allowance. Instead I hand him the money and feel my heart unclench a little. Whatever sins we commit as parents, and I've committed plenty, surely they can't be *that* bad if our children can't even remember them.

TURNING HEADS

———◦ıɐ◦———

AM I ALLOWED TO SAY THIS? I miss the wolf whistles.
I miss the double takes, the feeling of eyes on my back as
I move down a sidewalk, the "Hey, baby!" calls from a car rolling
past, windows cranked down and stereo cranked high and the guy
at the wheel holding out a big thumbs-up.

Oh, it still happens occasionally. But less and less. Often these
days I can walk through a crowd and feel something like . . .
invisible.

Before you get your feminist knickers in a twist, let me make
three points. The first is that if you had told my twenty- or thirty-
year-old self that I would (a) miss being catcalled and (b) admit
this publicly, she wouldn't have known where to begin telling you
that I had lost my mind. I was and remain a proud wearer of feminist knickers myself. The second point is that I'm not endorsing
men, or anyone, acting like horndog creeps. And the third is I'm
not claiming that I am now or ever was some total babe, a drop-
dead knockout. Cindy Crawford, Gisele Bündchen, whoever the
It girl du jour is—they can all rest easy tonight. My nose is too big

and my eyes are too small and I have weighed seven pounds more than I would like, just about every day of my adult life.

Still. Guys used to whistle. And now that they've mostly stopped, I miss it.

✳

MANY OF THE REFLECTIONS IN THIS BOOK ARE ABOUT SHIFTS UNDER WAY INSIDE MY HOME, OR INSIDE MY HEART. Interior shifts, not visible to the outside world. But it's hard to ignore that external ones are under way too. That how the world views and defines me is also changing.

In hindsight, there have been signs for a while that this was coming.

Exhibit A: the supermarket clerk, slouching in front of a notice that reads "We Card—NO EXCEPTIONS," as I try to pay for a bottle of wine. I'm fishing my driver's license out of my bag and he's already hit the override button on the register.

"No need, ma'am," he yawns. "You're all set."

I point to the sign. "What about 'no exceptions'?"

"We don't make seniors show ID. Next in line?"

Exhibit B: the reaction of my longtime hairdresser, when I announced that I might be ready for a radical change. "How about we switch things up from my natural blond?" I asked. It was autumn; the leaves were changing. I was craving boots and sweaters and pumpkin lattes and a magnificent mane of glossy, chestnut brown.

"I don't think so," he said gently. "Blond is so much more forgiving. My brunette clients have to come in every four weeks, to stay ahead of the gray roots."

"Sure, but I don't have that much gray yet. So maybe now's the time."

"Mm-hmm."

His eyebrows might have arched ever so briefly before he collected himself, handed me the new issue of *People* magazine, and proceeded to apply the exact same shade of highlights to my hair that he always does.

Exhibit C was an eager shop assistant, bustling up to the dressing room where I was trying on clothes. "How are we doing in here? Oh, that color is lovely with your skin! We've just gotten in some gorgeous new dresses. I'll bring a few. You still okay with showing your upper arms?"

Um, yes? Why wouldn't I be? Of all the body parts to feel self-conscious about, my upper arms seemed a weird one to bring up.

Sigh. That exchange in the dressing room was several years ago now. If you're reading this and having a similar reaction to her question, glancing down in confusion at your own shapely arms . . . I regret to report that you should enjoy them while you can. Go buy every tank top in sight. Wear them with gusto. Your future self and I are here to confirm that the jiggles will come for us all.

Most of this, honestly, I don't mind. I do wish my triceps were in a slightly less intimate relationship with gravity, but the rest of it—the gray hair, the crow's feet and laugh lines—I've earned them. I'm fine with looking my age. What has caught me by surprise is how uninterested the rest of the world seems in looking back. How very . . . *unseen* a woman of fifty can suddenly feel.

One of the more revelatory conversations I've had about this was with a girlfriend, close to my own age. She's the one who brought it up, having recently experienced a rite of passage that will be familiar to parents of teenagers. She and her firstborn were out for a walk, on the towpath beside the Potomac River, when they passed a boathouse. A men's varsity eight boat was docking. My friend felt eight sets of eyes on her. Heads turning. She straightened her shoulders and perked up—only to realize they were gawking not at her but at her teenager, ambling alongside.

She is both laughing and groaning as she tells me this story.

"First time that's happened. I'm sure it won't be the last. And listen, it's not that I want to be ogled by a bunch of random dudes half my age."

"No, of course not."

"Well. Maybe a little. But no, it's more that . . ." she pauses. "It's like I've lost a language I once spoke fluently."

I am intrigued because this particular friend is bilingual. She grew up in Europe. English is not her first language. She knows what it is to switch between tongues, to struggle to express yourself in one or the other. "Say more?" I prompt.

She talks about youth and beauty and how they confer power. How they inform how you move through the world, how you interact and communicate with others. "I still retain a few words," she says. "Like the odd tourist phrase or two. Enough to catch the drift of a passing conversation. But mostly it's gone now, forgotten."

I rush to assure her that she's still gorgeous. Not to mention brilliant and successful and adored by her friends and family.

"Yeah, yeah," she says. "You're kind. And thank you. I know how lucky I am. I know how superficial this might sound. But it feels like I have a giant 'Mom' sign tattooed on my head, like that's all people can see. Like I'm not a woman anymore, I am only a *mom*. And I miss what I once had, you know? It's like Kaia Gerber."

"Who?"

I must be overdue to see my hairdresser, because clearly I'm behind on *People* magazine. Which, if I had been keeping up, would have informed me that—speaking of people who've drawn their share of wolf whistles—Cindy Crawford has a daughter. A daughter who has grown up to be a supermodel too, who looks disconcertingly like her famous mom, minus the famous mole. When I get home from my friend's, I google the duo. Zillions of photos pop up. They show a mother and daughter side by side on the red carpet, or out shopping in Manhattan, or strolling and smiling at the beach. The two appear to be close. The photos also confirm that Crawford, well into middle age, remains singularly stunning.

And yet. Apparently even Cindy Crawford misses what she once had.

"I do," she told one interviewer, who asked if she sees herself in her daughter. "I always tease her, 'You have my old legs. Give them back.'"

✳

WHERE IS THE LINE BETWEEN WANTING TO LOOK GOOD AND WANTING TO LOOK YOUNG?

It is so ingrained that they are one and the same. That "young" equals good and old equals . . . well. Stroll the aisles of your local pharmacy and you'll find shelf after shelf packed with "anti-aging" serums and creams. An entire industry devoted to thwarting a natural process in which we are engaged, every last one of us, from the second we are born. An entire industry devoted to the proposition that aging is to be avoided, something to be *against*. As if . . . we have a choice?

Yes, of course, you can point to women who are dazzling in middle age and beyond. Hello, Helen Mirren. Hello, Salma Hayek and Catherine Deneuve and Emma Thompson and Iman. Women attractive not just *for their age*, but for any age, full stop. But if this is true—if mature women are indeed attractive, even dazzling—why do we see so little of them? Why is every ad campaign fronted by a seventeen-year-old? Why are the only billboards and TV commercials featuring mature women hawking either life insurance, Depend incontinence underwear ("Night Defense") or, you guessed it, anti-aging potions? Where are all the ads with older women enjoying a cold beer, or a sports car, or a sassy pair of jeans? Why are we so rarely shown images of older women . . . having *fun*?

It is hard not to come away with the message that our society is happy to revere and even celebrate mature women—it just doesn't want to look at them.

And talk to Katherine Clark if you think that message reverberates only in Hollywood and the beauty industry. Clark is one of the highest-ranking members of Congress, the assistant speaker of the U.S. House. In a recent Op-Ed for WBUR, Boston's NPR news station, she discussed her decision, a few years back, to stop dyeing her gray hair.

"Supporters pulled my staff aside and asked if I was ill," Clark wrote. Because why else would she let herself go? "People told me I would no longer be able to pass legislation, that I was throwing away my reputation as hard-working, and most confounding to me, that I would no longer be taken seriously by the public and my colleagues."

For real?

Can you imagine those comments being directed at a man?

Clark's piece does not delve into her views on wolf whistles. It does note, dryly, that America has somehow staggered on, despite being led "almost exclusively by gray-haired *men*" . . . for the last 250 years.

The Massachusetts congresswoman closes with a rallying cry: "Your hair should be whatever makes you feel happy, strong, or beautiful. Wear your decision with pride and as a challenge to any notion that women should be anything other than equal and empowered."

Absolutely. You go, girl. Sing it.

But if you want a reality check on how risky this can feel, just look to Clark's senior colleague. Nancy Pelosi is the Speaker of the House, second in line to succeed the president. Whatever your politics, you can admire the shrewdness that was required to claim her place running a club historically reserved for men. This is a woman keenly aware of what it takes to command power, and to hang onto it.

Pull up any recent photo of her. She is always elegant, always immaculately put together. She manages her image as skillfully as she manages her caucus. As of this writing, Pelosi is eighty-two years old. It is no accident that her hair is the same rich brown it's always been. Not a gray strand in sight.

I ASK TOUGH QUESTIONS FOR A LIVING.

The job of professional interviewer requires thinking through what exactly it is that you want to know, and then phrasing your question precisely to elicit that information. But it's actually the next step that requires more discipline: listening carefully to the answer and following up. You have to push. Not to trap or embarrass someone, but to try to understand what really matters to them, why they believe what they believe, and what evidence they can marshal to support their position.

The subject of wolf whistles would seem to present an opportunity to turn the tables and ask myself a tough question. Namely, what's really bothering me here? On my script before heading into the studio, I might type out a question something like this: "You say you're an empowered woman in the post-#MeToo era. You say men shouldn't act like horndog creeps. And yet . . . you miss catcalls? You want guys to yell 'Hey, baby' when they drive past? Ms. Kelly, how can all those statements simultaneously be true?"

"Excellent question," I might reply, playing for time. I might let the silence hang for a beat, or two or three. Because truly, how *can* I square those statements?

Maybe, I might eventually answer, maybe it boils down to this. The allure of youth is the promise of things fresh and supple, bright eyes and dewy cheeks and bodies still in bud. But it's also, at its most elemental, about possibility. About all the paths not yet taken, all the adventures yet to come. When you hit your forties and fifties, it can start to feel like more doors are closing than opening. You can start to wonder if the craziest, most joyful adventures are behind you.

Enter the guy in the muscle car, windows down and speakers thumping. Tires hot on asphalt, the chassis throbbing with the bass. *Boom boom boom boom.* Can you hear it? Can you see him?

He knows nothing's going to happen. You know nothing's going to happen. This isn't going anywhere; it doesn't need to. Everything that matters about this moment is already in motion. He's looking straight at you and for a split second you're all he sees.

This right here, people? This is the opposite of feeling invisible. You are seen. You exist. You are here. You are alive.

He whistles, and you can choose to be offended. Or you can choose to take it as an offering, a gift. I say, seize it. Whistle back if you like. Holler, "Hey, that's *Ms.* Baby to you!" if it makes you feel better. But take it. It's yours, all yours: this moment, this chance to square your shoulders and stare straight out at the world . . . and to feel it staring right back.

ZERO

———◦◦◦———

THIS IS THE CHAPTER I HAVE DREADED WRITING.

I have hinted that Alexander was a difficult delivery, that he was born sick. In fact, Alexander was born not alive.

There is a fat white envelope in his medical file that contains the details, an envelope that I had never opened. On the outside it is addressed simply to "Parents"; whoever was writing was too busy to look up our names. Underneath, in a different color ink, I have noted, "Discharge papers from NICU," the neonatal intensive care unit.

This envelope has rested in our file cabinet, sealed and undisturbed, since the day we brought him home. I don't remember throwing it in there. I must have been too exhausted to confront yet more hospital paperwork. Nick and I had spoken in person with Alexander's doctors and nurses; we had follow-up appointments galore scheduled with specialists. We knew he had suffered a stroke. We were focused on his recovery and treatment going forward. What was the point of torturing ourselves by looking back, reading a blow-by-blow account of the trauma that had unfolded on the day he was born?

Somehow fifteen years passed. It was only when I started digging around recently in Alexander's files, trying to find any documentation I'd kept about his speech therapy, that I found the envelope again. Curious, I tore it open. I naively figured I would flip through quickly, chuck it in the trash bin, and clear some space in the drawer. After all, what could it matter? We had survived this long without knowing what was in there.

The discharge summary begins benignly enough: "Baby boy Kelly is the 2930g product of a 38 1/7 wk gestation. . . ." The single-spaced pages are clotted with medical jargon. They describe a mostly non-eventful pregnancy, culminating with my being admitted to the hospital at 5:15 p.m. on a Saturday afternoon, contractions coming every five minutes. So far, so normal.

But from there the account turns dark. "Initial presentation was shoulder, and rotation was attempted," begins the section titled "Delivery History." This much I had known before reading. Alexander was breech, and a rare and especially dangerous type of breech, in which he had attempted to join the world shoulder first. The danger is that the shoulder gets stuck, and the mother's uterus—*my* uterus—keeps contracting over and over to surmount this obstacle, until the uterus ruptures. The delivery was further "complicated by nuchal cord x 2," meaning the umbilical cord was wrapped twice around his neck. They kept trying to rotate him. I kept begging for an epidural. When they lost his heartbeat ("nonreassuring fetal heart tones"), I was wheeled to an operating room for an emergency Cesarean section. The first attempt failed. He was stuck, too far engaged in the birth canal. The document is focused on the baby, but I had watched as they first split me open from hip to hip, then cut straight up my belly in a jagged, inverted "T" to try to lever him out.

It's here that my firsthand knowledge of events ends. Somewhere around this point I passed out, either from loss of blood or from pure horror. When I came to, hours later, I was in a recovery room and Alexander was in the NICU. He would remain there, in an incubator, for days. The dispassionate account in this long-forgotten envelope marks the first time I have learned specifics of the actual delivery.

"Patient was transferred to the warmer without respiratory effort, completely limp," it states. "Color initially noted as uniformly gray." Soon after, "there was one failed attempt at intubation."

The most devastating section, the one that causes my eyes to prick with tears all these years later, is titled "APGARs." The Apgar is a test given to newborns. It measures five things to check a baby's health: skin color, heart rate, reflexes, muscle tone, and respiration.

A perfect score is 10.

Alexander's, at one minute after delivery, was 0.

Zero.

No pulse, no response, not breathing.

M Y HANDS ARE SHAKING AS I READ THE CONTENTS OF THE ENVE-
LOPE, SHAKING AS I TYPE THIS NOW.

Which is intriguing, because there's no actual suspense here: I know how this story ends. Indeed, things start to look up even before the end of page one. Something called a BVM, a bag-valve-mask resuscitator, appears to have been crucial. Several minutes after delivery—exactly how many minutes is not clear—Alexander starts to fight to breathe. He is "stimulated vigorously" and CPAP (continuous positive airway pressure) is initiated, to try to keep his airway open. He falters, then keeps fighting. Things could go either way. "Irregular respiratory effort" is noted, as are "improved color, tone." They suction. More CPAP. By ten minutes after delivery, his Apgar score has soared to 7. Seven! Was there ever a more wondrous number in the history of numbers?

The "Delivery History" section closes with Alexander being transferred to the NICU, CPAP still in progress en route. Upon arrival, an IV is established. His blood pressure and head circumference are recorded. His length is "not yet measured"; there's been no time.

The comment that I keep running my finger over, the one that would have given me hope had I been conscious during those awful minutes, is this: "Good tone, pink all over body, strong cry."

Strong cry. Yep. Sounds just like him. My boy. He made it.

NOTHING ABOUT THE DAYS THAT FOLLOWED WAS EASY. I was weak and listless and would remain so for a while. We were permitted to visit the NICU but not to lift Alexander from the incubator. I was not allowed to hold him, not allowed to breastfeed.

In later sections, the discharge file discusses his stroke. "MRI on DOL 2 showed: 'Small, recent stroke at the border of the right thalamus and posterior limb of the right internal capsule,'" it reads. "The lesion measured approximately 6mm." In the hospital, they performed all kinds of tests trying to figure out what had caused it. Neither those test results nor any of the myriad pediatric neurology appointments in the months that followed revealed a satisfying answer. No one has ever been able to tell us how long Alexander went without a pulse, how long his brain had starved for oxygen. And we've never learned what was the cause and what was the effect. Did the stroke occur in utero and somehow contribute to his nightmare delivery, or was it the ordeal of his nightmare delivery that somehow caused a stroke?

These felt like urgent questions for a long time. They came into play when his speech was delayed. They flickered in my mind when he tripped, banged his head on concrete, and knocked out his front teeth at his third birthday party. And when he spiked a fever and a chest infection serious enough that the school nurse had occasion to track me down in Iraq. But as he grew and thrived, they loomed smaller. Whatever had happened at the border of the right thalamus and posterior limb of his right internal capsule . . . whatever injury his tiny head had sustained . . . it had healed. The neurologists eventually gave us the all clear. They could find no indication of lasting brain damage. No indication of anything other than a healthy kid. After a while I started writing "N/A" or "none" on routine health forms for sports and school when they asked about any significant medical history. None of this seemed like information that a summer camp counselor, about to instruct my son on how to pitch a tent or paddle a canoe, needed to know.

As I write this, Alexander sits upstairs in his bedroom at his desk. He is healthy. His skin glows pink and his heart beats and he breathes—in and out, over and over, without even having to try. His only cause for distress at this precise moment is an overload of Spanish homework. From the top of the kitchen stairs, he calls down: Will I come drill him on the difference between *ser* and *estar*? Also has anyone walked the dog? Also what's for dinner? I call back that I'll answer him when he asks me all this in Spanish.

It is difficult to reconcile the pages I have just read with the boy upstairs. They seem to chronicle an ancient history, one best folded away again and forgotten. But they are not irrelevant, not quite. First, because they cause my heart to fly out to the parents of children whose stories have a different outcome. The pain must be unending.

And second, they force me to think about the unthinkable.

I had known he was born sick. I had known—you had only to look at the ridge of scars bristling across my stomach—that his delivery had been far from ideal. But I had not fully understood, not until seeing my son reduced to a score of zero, how very close we came to losing him. I want to race upstairs, fold him in my arms, and never let him go. If I had known, if I had opened and read this envelope years ago, would I have let him out of my sight? Would I ever have left that little boy's side?

Because I did, so many times.

＊

THE TRIP THAT STANDS OUT IN THIS REGARD WAS TO PAKISTAN, IN 2006. I traveled to Islamabad and its twin city, Rawalpindi, then drove west to report from Peshawar and the Afghan border. The intelligence beat, then as now, involved trying to track the CIA, the NSA, and other spy agencies. This means paying attention to whatever they're paying attention to. In 2006, it boiled down mostly to two portfolios: terrorism and rising nuclear threats. The two converged in Pakistan.

"Pakistan has more terrorists per square mile than anyplace else on earth. And it has a nuclear weapons program that is growing faster than anyplace on earth. What could possibly go wrong?" Those are words I wrote for a fictional CIA officer to deliver in *Anonymous Sources*, my first novel, the one about an intrepid reporter named Alexandra James. I was able to write the lines with some confidence, drawing on my own reporting trips to Pakistan.

On the one in question, I had sat inside the headquarters of Pakistan's Inter-Service Intelligence agency, the ISI, and questioned the generals who ran it about allegations of links to the Taliban and Al Qaeda. They blew smoke rings above my head and denied the allegations. I sat inside the headquarters of the Strategic Plans Division, the SPD, and questioned the general in charge of Pakistan's nuclear arsenal about whether the weapons were locked down and safe. I don't remember if he blew smoke rings; I do remember what he said: yes.

Both the answers to my questions and the overall security situation grew less predictable outside the capital. My interpreter, a young woman from the country's troubled tribal areas, had for several days been by my side, helping me conduct interviews with her hair uncovered, earrings and necklaces flashing. But I remember the moment we left Islamabad and turned onto the Grand Trunk Road to make the two-hour drive to Peshawar. She fished a head scarf from her bag, wound it tightly to cover every feature but her eyes, and advised me to do the same. "Always, outside Islamabad," she whispered. We stopped along the way for tea and fruit with the leaders of the Akora Khattak madrassa, the famous religious school where many members of the Taliban had studied. We drove through Afghan refugee camps and then high into the mountains of the Khyber Pass. Another day, my interpreter took me to her family's village. We passed checkpoints to get there— many parts of the tribal areas were and remain no-go areas for foreigners and even for the Pakistani army—but we met no resistance. Men wandered up from their work in the sugarcane and tobacco fields and crowded around us. I asked about 9/11, and about bin Laden, whose whereabouts were then unknown.

"Osama can go to hell," one old man spat.

We stood in a muddy paddock and interviewed him and others until twilight fell, without a guard, without a cell phone, without having told anyone back in the office where we were. It was a phenomenal day of reporting. It challenged me to think more deeply about the complexities of the U.S.-Pakistan relationship. And it strikes me now, from a personal security perspective, as a pretty dumb thing to do.

The other thing that strikes me, as I comb back over NPR transcripts to recall who we talked to and where—is *when* this happened. I was away in Pakistan for the first two weeks of November 2006. James was three years old. Alexander was not yet thirteen months when I left. He was not yet walking. Hmmm. It occurs to me that I would think carefully even today, with my children nearly grown, before leaving my family to jet off for two weeks on assignment to—as a colleague based in Islamabad once described Pakistan—a "dysfunctional country, in a dangerous neighborhood, with nuclear weapons."

Do I regret going?

God, no.

Sharpen it to a more uncomfortable question: Do I regret having gone, now that I understand that Alexander had very nearly died only months before?

The answer, honestly, is still no.

And not just because he was totally fine, well cared for in my absence, and still crawling when I returned. I would be a different person, a different kind of mother, if I didn't get on that plane. Of course I would have hated it if I'd missed his first steps. But he would have been wriggling out of my lap even if I'd stayed. Squeezing him tight in my arms and never letting go—that was never an option, was it? Our children are outgrowing us from the moment they are born. You can let a lot of life pass you by, sitting at home, waiting for people to need you.

Tweak the question about regret by just a word or two, though, and the answer changes. I do not regret going. But do I regret leaving him? Yes. God, yes. Always. Still.

More than a dozen years later, as I departed for another

dysfunctional country with nuclear weapons, North Korea, I lingered at the door. Nick and the boys were inside the house, pottering about, debating whether to grill or order pizza for dinner. I tried to put words to what I felt. From the back seat of the car to the airport, I wrote the following on Twitter: "That moment, no matter how big your children get, when you're leaving on a long work trip & the taxi pulls up and your kids hug you & you just want to cancel the whole thing and go back inside & build a pillow fort instead."

Every damn time.

❈

BEFORE I LEFT FOR THAT 2006 TRIP TO PAKISTAN, I TAPED A PIECE OF PINK CONSTRUCTION PAPER TO THE DOOR IN JAMES'S BEDROOM. At the top I had glued a recent photo of myself, sunglasses pushed high on my head, smiling back over my shoulder. Beneath was a hand-drawn calendar, fourteen neat boxes. One for each day I would be gone. Inside each box was a smiley face or a heart or a short message ("Big kisses!" "Halfway done!"). The idea was that the boys would be reassured if they could keep track of my trip, by counting the days and crossing a big "X" over each one until Mommy came home.

I harbor deep suspicions that neither of them ever touched it. It must have been either the nanny or Nick who hastily crossed off every box, likely as I made my way back home from the airport, so I wouldn't get my feelings hurt. The Xs are too uniform, relentlessly within the lines. Not at all what a one-year-old or a three-year-old handed a black felt-tip pen would produce. I feel a pang of gratitude to whichever adult made that effort, followed by a pang of gentleness toward myself: I was trying so very hard.

Back in 2006, I had not yet grasped how fleeting a privilege it is to make a calendar like that. To believe that you stand so utterly at the center of another person's universe that they might care to count down the days, one by one, until you come home to them. Whereas if I were to travel tomorrow? My husband loves me, but he's not going to require a pink construction paper chart to survive two weeks without me. My teenagers love me, but ditto. My mother? My brother? My oldest, dearest friends? They would be fine with exchanging a flurry of pre-departure texts: "Have a great trip! Good luck! Stay safe!" I wish I could go back and tell myself, *Treasure this.* Treasure the way their eyes light up when you walk into a room. Treasure even the mornings they cry for you, the ones when you have to unwind and tear their arms from around your neck as you leave. Never again, I would tell my younger self—never again will someone need and love you with the intensity that James and Alexander do, right now.

I said that I dreaded writing this chapter, and I did. It is not easy to read or to write an account of your child in pain, even when the events in question are in the past tense and long ago. But corollary to the fact that you can't be in two places at once— that not one of us, not a single one, has figured out how to be on the Khyber Pass and be home building pillow forts at the same time—runs another reality.

It has to do with how two competing ideas can coexist. How two contradictory thoughts can both be true. Do I regret going? No. Do I regret leaving my babies? Yes.

I speak from personal experience when I say that the following holds true, whether children are newborns or nearly grown: it is possible both to hate leaving them, and to be terribly glad that you went.

WE WILL NOT BE INTIMIDATED

———•‡•———

"COME WITH ME," THE WOMAN SAYS, BECKONING. "Just you, not your colleagues." We are in the East Hall of the treaty room, on the seventh floor of the State Department. She works for the secretary of state. I am there to interview him. It is January 2020.

We have brought a team of five from the newsroom: me, my producer, my editor, a writer from our digital team, plus NPR's longtime diplomatic correspondent Michele Kelemen. The interview had begun cordially.

"Good to see you," I say.

"Good to be with you," replies Secretary Mike Pompeo. "Thanks for having me on the show."

"Let's start with Iran."

I never share my questions in advance. But it is common practice for the staff of public figures to inquire as to what broad topics you intend to cover. With a sitting secretary of state, there are a thousand things you want to ask, a thousand possible lines of questioning. I had been chasing an interview with Pompeo for months. At various points, depending on what was dominating the headlines, I had pitched conversations focused on China, Turkey, Syria, Ukraine, and Iran. On this cold January morning, though, he is granting me ten minutes only. Much better to try to elicit a meaningful back-and-forth on one or two subjects than to attempt to cram in everything.

Iran was the obvious starting point. That month had seen the United States and Iran step to the brink of war. I'd actually been in Iran, covering the fallout of the U.S. assassination of Iranian general Qassem Soleimani, when word came that my interview request for Pompeo was confirmed. My producer, photographer, and I had walked behind Soleimani's casket through the streets of Tehran, where hundreds of thousands of mourners had converged for the funeral. Many were vowing revenge; some held signs reading "Down with USA" and "Hey US! You Started, We Will End It." We talked with as many of them as we could, asking what form this revenge might take. I put the same question, while in Tehran, to Pompeo's counterpart, Iran's then foreign minister Javad Zarif. He told me Soleimani's killing amounted to an act of war. He vowed that Iran would respond "according to our own timing and choice." He also acknowledged, ominously, that Iran was suspending compliance with the centrifuge limits on its nuclear program, and, in a separate part of the interview, he accused Pompeo of threatening to starve Iranians and called this a "crime against humanity."

Two days later, the State Department had reached out.

"I've got time on the secretary's schedule for an interview with you!" came the email from an aide in the Global Public Affairs office.

By the time Pompeo and I sat down, back in Washington, an uneasy pause had taken hold. The United States and Iran appeared, for the moment, to have stepped back from the brink. I wanted to focus on two questions: What path, if any, did the secretary see for diplomacy with Iran? It had occurred to me to wonder whether swapping insults through journalists like me might be as close as the top diplomats of the United States and Iran had come to communicating during the crisis. My other central question was: How did the U.S. plan to prevent Iran from getting a nuclear weapon, should it decide to do so? We went around on that one for a while:

> KELLY: But my question again, how do you stop Iran from getting a nuclear weapon?

> POMPEO: We'll stop them.

> KELLY: How? Sanctions?

> POMPEO: We'll stop them.

He declined to elaborate. Still, Pompeo was keen to continue talking about Iran. Indeed, if he had had his druthers, that's all we would have talked about. Katie Martin, the public affairs officer who handled media for Pompeo, had written to me the night before the interview to drive home the point.

"Know you just got back from Tehran so we would like to stick to Iran as the topic as opposed to jumping around. Is that something we can agree to?"

Nope, I wrote back. "I am indeed just back from Tehran and plan to start there. Also Ukraine. And who knows what the news gods will serve up overnight. I never agree to take anything off the table."

I did agree to spend a "healthy portion" of my allotted ten minutes on Iran, and I did—more than two-thirds of the final interview. But recall that January 2020 was not only the month the United States nearly went to war in the Middle East, it was also the month that the Senate began an impeachment trial of the president of the United States, over charges to do with Ukraine. Pompeo was in charge of U.S. foreign policy. He was one of the few people who'd actually been on the infamous July 25, 2019, phone call between President Trump and the president of Ukraine (the "I would like you to do us a favor" call, the call that set the whole impeachment saga in motion). State Department officials who worked for Pompeo, including the ousted ambassador to Ukraine, Marie Yovanovitch, had appeared as star witnesses at the impeachment hearings. There was no universe in which questions about Ukraine were inappropriate; there was no way a serious journalist would sit down with Pompeo in that moment and *not* ask about it.

"Change of subject," I said, after six minutes and thirty-seven seconds of increasingly tense back-and-forth with the secretary of state on Iran. "Ukraine. Do you owe Ambassador Marie Yovanovitch an apology?"

Pompeo and I were seated facing each other, in the center of the room. My colleagues had taken seats beside a window; his team had lined up their chairs against the wall behind him. He said he did not want to talk about Ukraine but then, despite himself, he did. With about a minute left on the clock, Katie Martin stopped the interview. "Thank you," she said, politely but firmly, leaving no doubt that we were done and I would not be getting my full ten minutes with the secretary. I thanked him, twice. He did not reply. He stood, leaned very close, and glared at me. Then he turned and, with his staff, left the room.

A minute or two later, as my team and I were packing up, Martin reappeared.

"Come with me." She summoned me back to the secretary's

private living room. Just me, no microphone or recorder, though she did not say we were off the record, nor would I have agreed.

That's when things took an unusual turn.

※

A S A PARENT, YOU TRY TO PASS ON YOUR VALUES.
You hope to instill in your children ideals to live up to, share lessons you've learned along the way. It's hard to gauge how much your kids take in. Are they listening, when you preach about the importance of kindness? When you tell them for the thousandth time how fortunate they are, and that yes, they really do have to write that thank-you note? I believe that while they may not always listen to what we say, they do watch what we do. How we, their parents, navigate the world.

I write now about the interview with Pompeo with an eye to what I learned from it, and also to what I hope James and Alexander might take away from it, from watching their mother at work. Three ideas stand out. The first is so basic, so simple, and yet so hard on many days to live up to: never give up.

In the context of a newsmaker interview, it means holding your ground. You ask a question, and if they don't answer it, or if they answer it in an incomplete or unsatisfying or confusing way, you ask again. And again. Don't let them dodge it. Don't let them change the subject or spin the conversation toward their preferred talking points. Be ready with facts to test their argument. Don't give up. It's not that they owe me, Mary Louise Kelly, anything. It's that I'm there as a surrogate for millions of NPR listeners, people who may never get the chance to put questions directly to our nation's leaders. Sometimes, when an interview turns contentious and it would be easier just to move on to the next topic, I can feel all those people lined up behind me. They're right there, over my shoulder. An army, an almost physical presence, packed tight and straining to listen, muttering, "But what about . . . ?" They deserve answers.

It's difficult sometimes to know how hard to push. There's a fine line between being rigorous and being obnoxious, between being persistent and being an ass. I often think of the British journalist Jeremy Paxman, a master at walking right up to that line, dangling his feet over the edge, and calling, "Yoo-hoo!" before pulling back at the last possible second. Paxman famously asked the same question twelve times in a 1997 BBC interview with Britain's home secretary. That's right, twelve times. The topic was the sacking of the UK prisons chief, and while the interview veered at times into the weeds of British domestic politics, the famous question itself was a straightforward one: "Did you threaten to overrule him?"

"I did not overrule him," Michael Howard replies.

"Did you *threaten* to overrule him?"

"I took advice on what I could or could not do—"

"Did you threaten to overrule him, Mr. Howard?"

The exchange is tough but courteous. It's also utterly compelling to watch, not least because Paxman is so clearly enjoying himself.

"I'll note you're not answering the question, whether you threatened to overrule him. . . ." That's attempt number nine.

By number ten, he allows himself a chuckle. "It's a yes-or-no question!" he says, shaking his head and smiling. "A yes-or-no answer!"

Paxman never does extract a yes or a no from the home secretary. But I would argue there's value here in watching Howard squirm, a thing I do not write lightly. I'm not in this line of work to embarrass people or to score political points. I do not relish confrontation. But government officials—people whose salaries are paid by us, the taxpayers—should be prepared to answer reasonable questions about their actions. In a democracy, it falls to journalists to pose these questions. And Paxman's interview style is instructive, in that the nonanswer to a simple inquiry, posed over and over, was far more revealing and memorable than a more intricate string of questions could have produced.

In my interview with Mike Pompeo, I did not ask the same question a dozen times. That's a standard to which I'll have to continue to aspire. But in the truncated Ukraine portion of the conversation, I did push, again and again, on one thing: the administration's treatment of Ambassador Yovanovitch. Her credentials and reputation were impeccable, yet she was undermined, threatened, smeared, and ultimately recalled from Kyiv. I was genuinely curious about how Pompeo would defend it. He dodged my first question ("I agreed to come on your show today to talk about Iran"). But remember, it wasn't just me asking. I could feel others, perched just over my shoulder, heads cocked to listen. An entire generation of Foreign Service Officers, both current and former, were furious with Pompeo for failing to defend Yovanovitch and other diplomats. Pompeo's own senior adviser Michael McKinley had testified, under oath, that this failure was a factor in his decision to resign. If Pompeo wouldn't answer me, would he answer Ambassador McKinley?

POMPEO: I'm not going to comment on things that Mr. McKinley may have said. I'll say only this. I have defended every State Department official. We've built a great team. The team that works here is doing amazing work around the world.

KELLY: Sir, respectfully, [crosstalk] where have you defended Marie Yovanovitch?

POMPEO: I've defended every single person on this team. I've done what's right for every single person on this team. [crosstalk]

KELLY: Can you point me toward your remarks where you have defended Marie Yovanovitch?

POMPEO: I've said all I'm going to say today. Thank you. Thanks for the repeated opportunity to do so. I appreciate that.

KELLY: One further question on this.

Actually, I got in two more questions before they stopped the interview. I have to smile, reading the transcript now. The sarcasm ("Thanks for the repeated opportunity") is impressive. And the nonanswer to a simple question is, as always, revealing.

I don't know if James and Alexander have ever listened to my interview with Pompeo. I've never asked. If and when they do, what I hope they hear is my determination. Their mom, in close conversation with a powerful man, following up, pushing back, not quitting. I hope they hear a sincere effort to ask questions on behalf of my fellow citizens. And then to share the answers—or lack thereof—with the world.

IN THE PRIVATE LIVING ROOM THAT ADJOINS HIS OFFICE, POMPEO WAS WAITING FOR ME. Three people were present for what happened next: Katie Martin, who had ushered me back there. The secretary of state. And me.

He was standing before a window. A bowl of red, white, and

blue "#SWAGGER" lapel buttons was set out on display, a nod to his campaign to help the State Department "get its swagger back."

Pompeo proceeded to shout at me for about the same amount of time as the interview itself had lasted. He was not happy to have been asked about Ukraine. He insisted that I had promised to question him only about Iran. I said that was incorrect, that it was my consistent practice over decades of journalism never to consent to taking a topic off the table. I pointed out that I had confirmed in writing my specific intention to ask about Ukraine, via email to Martin the night before.

"I don't care what you agreed with my fucking staff."

He went on, "Do you think Americans care about fucking Ukraine?"

Yes, I did.

"Could you even find Ukraine on a fucking map?"

He opened a pair of double doors and called for aides to bring a map of the world. They delivered one. A strange map, with no writing on it, no countries marked, no international borders drawn. Just gray blobs of continents and oceans. I pointed to Ukraine. He put the map away. He said, "People will hear about this."

I agreed that they would, since we planned to air the interview that same day. Then he turned and said he had things to do. I thanked him again for his time and left.

It was not yet ten o'clock. Our sister program, *Morning Edition*, was on air. Our plan going in had been that if Pompeo made news, we would race a clip or two onto that show, then broadcast the full interview that afternoon on *All Things Considered*. At 10:07 a.m., I went live from the State Department. NPR maintains a tiny bureau there, a closet really, near the press briefing room. Just enough space for a couple of chairs and a work surface for a computer, microphone, and broadcast gear. With the help of my producer, who had already uploaded the tape to servers at NPR headquarters, and my editor, who had dashed off a rough script, I updated *Morning Edition* with the highlights of what Pompeo had said on Iran. I also played a long chunk of the Ukraine portion of the interview.

The next several hours brought multiple, intense discussions with editors back in the newsroom over whether and how to report what had happened in Pompeo's private living room. At some point that day, I went to our CEO John Lansing to let him know what was going on. Among the questions we all debated: What news value would it add? How would it advance our listeners' knowledge of U.S. foreign policy, always a primary goal of any State Department interview? And what if Pompeo denied it? I would find myself in a he-said, she-said tiff with the secretary of state. There was only one other witness to the encounter—and she worked for him.

What swayed me in the end was a rule that I've heeded through many a conundrum in the news business: when in doubt, just say what you know and how you know it. People can make up their own minds what they want to think about it. This entire interview was on the record. The map-test portion was indisputably newsworthy; it spoke to Pompeo's stewardship of the State Department. It spoke to how little the administration seemed to value the relationship with Ukraine, a relationship that was then dominating the national conversation. And it felt important for Americans to glimpse how America's most senior diplomat—the man charged with steering our nation's foreign policy—conducted himself behind closed doors.

I reached out again to the State Department, told them we planned to report the screamed obscenities and the map test, and asked if they wanted to provide any further comment or context.

All that night, as the interview aired from coast to coast and was picked up by news outlets around the world, they did not.

But the following morning, a Saturday, on official letterhead bearing the State Department seal, Pompeo issued a statement. He did not deny anything in my account. Here is the statement, in full:

> NPR reporter Mary Louise Kelly lied to me, twice. First, last month, in setting up our interview and, then again yesterday, in agreeing to have our post-interview conversation off the record. It is shameful that this reporter chose to violate the basic rules of journalism and decency. This is another example of how unhinged the media has become in its quest to hurt President Trump and this Administration. It is no wonder that the American people distrust many in the media when they so consistently demonstrate their agenda and their absence of integrity.
>
> It is worth noting that Bangladesh is NOT Ukraine.

I can confirm the accuracy of one sentence and one sentence only. The last one. Bangladesh is most certainly not Ukraine.

I WAS ALONE, SIPPING COFFEE AT MY KITCHEN TABLE, WHEN THE STATE- MENT FROM POMPEO LANDED IN MY INBOX. As NPR's correspondent assigned to cover the State Department, Michele Kelemen was on an internal distribution list and had received it first. She forwarded it to me with a brief note: "Did you know this was coming?"

I did not.

I read it and then read it again. The last sentence bewildered me. It took a few seconds to grasp what he was implying, that I had confused Ukraine with Bangladesh, a country on an entirely different continent, thousands of miles away. I couldn't in that moment think of a constructive response other than to push back from the table, lace up my sneakers, and head outside for a run. It helped. When I returned and checked Twitter, I saw that tens of thousands of people had followed me in the brief window that I'd been offline. Interview requests from the major TV networks and cable news were flooding in. One by one, I turned them down. I wanted the interview and our journalism to stand on their own.

This gets at the second lesson I hope my boys might take from this episode, which is that you can control only your own actions. You can control what you do but not, alas, what others do. This is such a hard one. When someone treats me poorly, my first impulse is not to rise serenely above it, but to punch back. I wrestle with my better angels daily. And I see the boys wrestle with theirs; they'll come home from school raging about some injustice, some perceived slight. "It's not fair!" they seethe, and this is both usually true and nearly always a moot point.

It rankled to decline all those interview requests. I had plenty I would have liked to say. But I wanted to cover the news, not be the news. I didn't want to fan the flames. And the only person whose actions I could control . . . was me.

In the days that followed, some news outlets ran with the narrative of a feud between Pompeo and NPR. The narrative gained currency when Kelemen, who was scheduled to travel as the radio pool reporter on Pompeo's next overseas trip, was told she was no longer welcome on the plane. The itinerary for the trip had been finalized before he sat down with me, and it featured a stop (Department of You Can't Make This Stuff Up) in Ukraine. For the record, I have no feud with Mike Pompeo. I wish him well. Same for his aide Katie Martin, who struck me as smart, loyal to her boss, and caught in an impossible situation.

What did bother me about Pompeo's statement—the part that had me struggling to hold my tongue—was his broad swipe at the press overall. His comments about how "unhinged the media has become," and about "their absence of integrity." This was an attack not just on me and my journalism, which he was free not to like, but on all journalists.

It was beneath the dignity of his office. And I felt it more keenly coming from him than I would have coming from, say, the Treasury secretary. It is the explicit job of the secretary of state to uphold and promote American values worldwide, including freedom of the press. It is not the secretary of state's job, on the other hand, to administer geography pop quizzes, to berate a reporter for asking questions he doesn't like, or to retaliate against another reporter—the respected and deeply experienced Kelemen—by kicking her off his plane, for no reason other than that she worked for the same news organization I did.

But I couldn't control his decisions. Only mine. The best course of action, I decided, was to put my head down, report for work, and do my job.

"Looking forward to committing some excellent journalism," I tweeted on that first weekday back in the newsroom. "Have a great Monday, everyone." On the show that afternoon, I did not mention Mike Pompeo. Instead, I interviewed Independent senator Angus King of Maine about whether the Senate should call witnesses in President Trump's impeachment trial. I spoke with our Beijing correspondent about a mysterious new virus that had originated in Wuhan, China. I interviewed our immigration reporter about a Supreme Court ruling that had just dropped, and another colleague, just back from the Sundance Film Festival, on which buzzy movie premieres to watch for.

It turns out that being a mother was the perfect preparation for navigating this surreal situation. I did not have experience with being sworn at and called a liar by the secretary of state of the United States of America. But I had plenty of directly relevant experience, from handling a toddler throwing a tantrum. You learn not to dignify the behavior with a response.

✳

IT WAS ALAN DERSHOWITZ, LONGTIME PROFESSOR AT HARVARD LAW SCHOOL, WHO PUSHED ME OVER THE EDGE.

Four days after my sit-down with Pompeo, Dershowitz turned up at a White House event to mark the unveiling of a new plan for the Middle East. This in itself was not noteworthy. Dershowitz has represented clients of all political stripes over his career. He describes himself as a liberal Democrat, but he had become prominent in Trump's orbit, and had signed on with the team of lawyers defending the president at what would become his first impeachment trial. Dershowitz's role was to deliver part of the opening statement, the part presenting what he saw as the constitutional case against impeachment.

At the White House event, Dershowitz was seated in the row behind Pompeo, a circumstance captured by television cameras when the president departed from his script to praise Pompeo. Specifically, to praise him for verbally attacking me.

"Very impressive, Mike," Trump said. "That reporter couldn't have done too good a job on you yesterday. I think you did a good job on her, actually."

The audience applauded. Dershowitz laughed, leaned forward, and patted Pompeo approvingly on the back. As I watched from my desk in the newsroom, something in me snapped. Not because of Trump's comments. It is jarring, of course, to listen as the president of the United States publicly praises another man for doing "a good job" on you. But by that point in his tenure, Trump's views on "fake news" were well documented. No surprise that he would denigrate and mock the press. Nor was it a surprise that Pompeo would laugh along. He was known for aligning himself with his boss to a degree unusual even among members of Trump's cabinet. In the *New Yorker*, journalist Susan Glasser had quoted a former American ambassador who memorably described Pompeo as "like a heat-seeking missile for Trump's ass." It was almost—almost—enough to make you feel sorry for the guy.

But Dershowitz! I had just interviewed him, by phone, exactly one week before I sat down with Pompeo. I'd pressed him on his role at the impeachment trial, and also on his ties to the convicted and imprisoned sex offender Jeffrey Epstein, who had recently either killed himself or been murdered, depending on which account you believed. Dershowitz had been Epstein's attorney. He told me he was "very proud" of it. Could questions about that relationship prove a distraction and get in the way of his making an effective case for Trump? We had a calm, civil back-and-forth about it. What about the allegations from one of Epstein's accusers, targeting Dershowitz himself and claiming that she had been made to have underage sex with him? We had a remarkably civil back-and-forth about that too, with Dershowitz stating that he had disproven those allegations "categorically" and briefly describing how. My point being, it's possible to engage in civil back-and-forth on the most uncomfortable of subjects, if both interviewer and guest are prepared to operate from a baseline of mutual respect.

I'd never met Dershowitz personally. But I had long looked up to him. He was now a professor emeritus and had been an institution at Harvard, where I was an undergrad. He was my father's law school professor in the 1970s. Two decades later, he had taught the man who would become my husband. He had always been brilliant, and provocative; I had listened to Dershowitz stories at the family dinner table since I was a little girl. It stung to watch him now, toadying at the White House, chortling at my expense. But Dershowitz, it emerges, taught Pompeo too.

"He's my former student," Dershowitz said in an interview with the right-wing Newsmax channel. "Of course I'm going to pat him on the back and congratulate him for the work he has done."

In a separate, earlier interview on CNN, when challenged on why he'd chosen that *exact* moment to pat and congratulate his former protégé, Dershowitz had elaborated. "I don't think reporters should ever be treated that way," he said of me. "But I like Mike Pompeo's views on the Middle East. . . . And if he can help bring about peace in the Middle East, I'll forgive him his rudeness towards a reporter."

You know what? I agree. No hard feelings. If bawling out a reporter helps get a guy in the right frame of mind to cement peace in the Middle East, count me in. Happy to take one for the team. Map tests ahoy!

In seriousness, though—and setting aside the fact that Pompeo fared no better at bringing lasting peace to the Middle East than any of the secretaries of state who have come before or since—I was starting to wonder if attempting to float serenely above the fray was going to be enough, or if it was time to speak up. Not to settle scores. And certainly not to prolong my minor turn in the spotlight; I was really, *really* ready for the news cycle to move on. But watching Dershowitz, watching that whole room of mostly men snickering away, I decided that I had something to say. I'd already been noodling whether to write something to refocus attention on the substance of my conversation with Pompeo, and for that matter my earlier conversation with his Iranian counterpart, both of which had been overshadowed by the hullabaloo. NPR was the only news organization to have sat down that month with the top diplomats of both Iran and the United States, in their respective capitals, as the two countries lurched toward and then backed off from armed confrontation. That alone felt worth reflecting on.

A few hours after the Trump-Pompeo-Dershowitz chucklefest at the White House, I pitched an Op-Ed piece to the *New York Times*. I wanted it to run there both to reach people outside the United States—the *Times* boasts an impressive number of international readers—and to dispel any notion that this was some Pompeo-versus-NPR vendetta. No. Something bigger was at stake.

That same night, my piece went live, bearing the headline "Pompeo Called Me a 'Liar.' That's Not What Bothers Me."

J AMES AND ALEXANDER, IF THERE IS ONE LAST LESSON THAT I HOPE YOU TAKE FROM ANY OF THIS, IT'S ABOUT THE NECESSITY, SOME-TIMES, OF STANDING UP TO BULLIES. This is generally neither fun nor easy. (It has that in common with the other two takeaways I have thrown your way, about never giving up and about owning your actions.) But when I look back over my life to date, I can think of occasions when I regret not having stood up to someone or something. I can think of none I regret that went the other way, not a single time I was sorry to have found my voice and used it.

I do need to recognize the chutzpah of lecturing either of you on standing up to a bully, when one of the most exuberant examples I've ever seen was the two of you in action. Alexander, you were very small, not yet three years old. James was five and about to start a new school for kindergarten. I thought it would be fun to drive over and check out the sandbox and swings setup, so that James would already have his bearings at recess on the first day. Other families must have had a similar idea; the playground was busy. A posse of big kids, meaning rising first and second graders, had staked out the grass around the big slide. James, ever social and outgoing, ran over and started chattering. But they didn't know him, and he was the new kid and didn't know the rules of whatever game they were playing, and they began to taunt him. It escalated when one of them told James to go away and underscored the point by giving him a shove.

I was about to intervene when you launched yourself.

"My brother," you said, and I was amazed because you still didn't talk much at that point. "My brother," you repeated, and your head went down and you ran at the shover-in-chief. Your sweaty little skull aimed straight and hard into his stomach. A human battering ram.

The kid toppled back onto his bum. He looked at me, eyes wide with shock: *You're a mom, aren't you going to do something?* James stared at you: *What the heck just happened?* A question already overtaken by events because now you were climbing on top of the kid, elbows flying, trying to pull his hair. I didn't need to see your eyes to know the question in them: *You ready to apologize and beg for mercy or do I need to continue?*

I waded in just as other moms took notice and came running. "Upsy-daisy!" I pulled the child upright. "Now, Gunther." Was his name Gunther? He looked like a Gunther. "There's a good boy. Sorry about your tummy. You okay? This is James. He's starting school here next week! And this is Alexander." Gunther flashed a look of panic. "He's nice. I promise. Just maybe don't shove his brother again, okay?"

When we got back to the car, James asked, "Is Alexander in trouble?"

"Do you think he should be?"

"No. I think he was protecting me."

"Me too. Fighting is bad. But if somebody shoves your brother, you stand up for him. Should we go home and make afternoon snack?"

I glanced in the rear-view mirror. Alexander, you were staring placidly out the window. The look of a little boy whose work is done. By the time we got home, you were fast asleep, your sweaty, almost certainly sore head drooping against the wide straps of your car seat.

Over the years, Nick and I have had all the usual Responsible Parent chats with you boys, about seeking out a teacher when you need help, and about using your words. But I'll be honest: I was brimming with pride that day at the playground. I'm not condoning schoolyard brawls. And I'll concede this doesn't quite line up with my earlier seize-the-moral-high-ground kumbaya thoughts on controlling your own actions and rising serenely above the fray. (In your defense, you were *two*. You didn't have a lot of other conflict resolution strategies in your arsenal yet, so you opted for the tried-and-true method, nailing your adversary with a sucker punch to the gut.)

The thing about life is that it's complicated. It throws you choices where holding true to one cherished value puts you in conflict with another. When you're not sure what to do, I recommend asking yourself that question again: Which choice would you be able to defend to a child? Which choice will allow your eighty-year-old self to sleep easy at night? I'll bet good money that you land on the one where you lower your head, take aim, and run straight at a bully tormenting someone or something that you love.

✳

I'VE SAID THAT I TURNED DOWN ALL INTERVIEW REQUESTS. This is true. But my boss, John Lansing, did not. He accepted one. The day that Pompeo dropped his "Bangladesh is NOT Ukraine" statement, NPR's CEO took questions from my colleague Michel Martin. She anchors *All Things Considered* on the weekends and, bless her, she does not mess around. Michel (no relation to Katie Martin at State) made clear at the top that her team had asked for the interview because they're trained to book stakeholders in a news story, not because some NPR exec thought it might be good spin. This is one of the things I love about working for NPR: when circumstances demand, we cover ourselves just as we would any other company. Reporting by journalists in the newsroom, *about* our newsroom, is firewalled from the public relations team and other execs. Not every media company does this; vanishingly few would put their own CEO on air, taking questions that have not been pre-screened or vetted in any way.

Michel asked Lansing for his response to Pompeo calling me a liar. ("I stand behind her. And I stand behind the NPR newsroom. And the statement from the secretary of state is blatantly false.") She asked whether gender might have been a factor in Pompeo's expletive-laced rage. (Lansing: "I can't say that for sure. But whether it was aimed at a woman or a man, it was outrageous and inappropriate.") Finally, she asked for context. Just how far outside the range of normal was this interview?

For someone who may run a news organization but who does not often have occasion to find himself behind a hot mic, Lansing was refreshingly direct.

"It's not unusual for there to be tension between government officials and journalists because journalists are—as I said, their duty is to ask difficult questions," he replied. "But this goes well beyond tension. This goes towards intimidation. And let me just say this. We will not be intimidated."

Thank you, I breathed, listening at home. I hadn't been given any input into the questions either; I didn't know what Michel would ask or how our boss would answer until the interview aired nationwide. Lansing's words were reassuring. They were galvanizing, because Lansing spoke not just for himself but on behalf of our entire organization. In that moment, it's fair to say he was speaking for the entire Fourth Estate as we worked to cover the Trump administration: "We will not be intimidated." Lansing's message prompted me to consider that while my interaction with Pompeo might have been bizarre, it had not been scary. How different might it have felt if I were a freelancer? If I hadn't had the editorial and legal muscle of a major news network behind me? How different might it have felt if I were a reporter living and working in a country with no codified protections for the press, a country where challenging a senior official can land you in prison or worse? Answer: it would have felt terrifying.

I had all that in my head when I sat down to write for the *Times*.

"Ask journalists why they do the job they do," I began, "and you'll hear a range of answers. Here's mine: Not every day, but on the best ones, we get to put questions to powerful people and hold them to account. This is both a privilege and a responsibility."

I wrote about the interviews I'd done in Tehran and in Washington. I wrote about how that month, the risk of miscalculation—of two old adversaries misreading each other and accidentally escalating into war—had felt very real. I wrote that the stakes were too high for the impulses and decisions of Tehran's and Washington's top policymakers not to be examined in as thoughtful and unflinching an interview as possible. I wrote about why it matters that freedom of the press is enshrined in the U.S. Constitution. *Use your words*, we had taught the boys. I was trying, in my way, to use my words, to explore whether it is possible at the same time both to take the high road . . . and to tilt headfirst at a bully.

Did my speaking up make any difference? In one sense, absolutely not. If anything, the Trump administration saw out 2020 with a more energetic assault on fact-based reality than it had begun the year. The Big Lie begat the January 6 insurrection; in his remarks that day on the Ellipse, urging his supporters to march on the U.S. Capitol, Trump twice called the media "the enemy of the people." The media, he added, is "the biggest problem we have in this country." That afternoon a mob of the president's supporters attacked and ransacked the Capitol. Five people died. In the days that followed, Pompeo did not distance himself from his boss. He declined to protest or even to acknowledge Trump's role in inciting the violence. And to my knowledge, he never did apologize to Marie Yovanovitch, or to any of the other State Department officials whose careers were derailed by shadow back-channel diplomacy on Ukraine or by the subsequent impeachment trial.

Still, as my colleague Peter Sagal is fond of saying, if you have a bigger platform than most people, you bear some responsibility to use that platform to benefit those other people. I have a bigger platform than most people. And sometimes it matters less what you say than the mere fact that you are speaking up. You never know who might be listening.

Toward the end of that very, very long week, toward the end of the workday, one of the younger producers on the show came to find me in the studio.

"Hi," he said. "Got a sec?"

I was packing up, logging off, exhausted, beyond ready to head home and pour a glass of wine.

"Of course." I sank back down into my chair and steeled myself. "What's up?" *What now?*

He cleared his throat. "I just wanted to say I'm proud to work here. Proud to be a journalist. This"—he swept his arm around, to indicate the studio and the newsroom beyond—"I mean, everything that's happened these last few days, this is what I came to journalism to do."

"Oh! I didn't—I wasn't expecting that. I'm so glad. It's been quite the learning experience. For all of us."

"Sure has."

"And you're right. This is what we came to do."

SHOWING UP

————•••————

O N THE WEEKENDS, I LIKE TO GO FOR A LONG RUN. Five miles, ten. Sometimes farther, if I'm training for something in particular. I run slowly, and I run alone. This is my time. No music, no podcasts. Just me and my thoughts, breathing hard, ticking down the miles, escaping stress and obligation and my generally frazzled state of existence.

I keep the running app open on my phone to log my distance, but I close and mute everything else: texts and email and Twitter and Instagram and Slack, all of it. If you really need me, you'll have to pick up the phone and call. And even then I probably won't answer, unless you are one of my children.

This is how I came to answer the phone on a recent Sunday morning in Georgia. I grew up there. My family is still there. It's an easy trip from DC, and I had flown down on my own for the weekend to celebrate my baby brother's birthday. In Atlanta, I have a few favorite jogging routes that I rotate, depending on the weather, the time of day, and how long I can spare. This morning I've picked one that proceeds from my parents' front door past the Cathedral of St. Philip, where I grew up going to Sunday school and once played the Virgin Mary in the children's Christmas pageant. Then a left turn, to trot along busy Peachtree Road for a mile or so, and then another left, down West Paces Ferry, past the Governor's Mansion and along to OK Cafe, an old-school diner that makes a mean grilled cheese. It's not the most tranquil route. You're pounding concrete sidewalks for most of it, running alongside traffic, and there are a few long lights where you can get caught and be forced to jump up and down in place while waiting an eternity for the walk sign. But it's flat and familiar and I like to see what's changed since the last time I was home. This particular morning, I'm a mile or so into my planned seven-mile loop, when my phone rings and I glance down and see that it is James.

"Hey, sweet boy!" I pant. "Hang on." I jog out of the road and onto the edge of someone's front yard. Dew still wet on the grass, red clay poking up from the flower beds, slender pine trees thickening into a canopy above. "How are you? Get a good sleep last night?"

"Hi, Mom. Can you move Dad's car?"

"What?"

"It's blocking me."

In Washington, we have room for three cars on our driveway if we scrunch, but they're tandem spaces. It's a constant shuffle. Whoever gets home first at night is screwed trying to pull out the next morning. Often I end up parking on the street, even when my own driveway is completely empty, to spare myself the hassle of getting trapped.

"Um, James. No. I can't move Dad's car."

"*Mom!* I have the SAT tutor! I have to leave right now! Why can't you—"

"I can't move Dad's car because I'm not home. I'm not in Washington. I'm in Georgia, remember? For Uncle C.J.'s birthday?"

Silence.

"Fine, I'll find Dad."

The line goes dead.

I stand staring at the phone in my hand. James's call prompts two questions. The second one is, Why didn't he go find his father in the first place if the issue is his father's car? (Answer: mothers truly do remain the default for everything.) But this question won't occur to me until later, because I'm too stricken by the first one: Had he actually not noticed I was gone? Had he not missed me . . . at all?

Today is Sunday. I left Washington on Friday morning. This is day three. It has not crossed my son's mind to wonder where I was at breakfast, or why I haven't been nagging him about curfew, or why it's been dark and silent in my study, the one he walks past multiple times a day, because it lies between his bedroom and the kitchen. Only four people live in our house; I like to think I would notice if one of them disappeared for a few days.

This is the same child for whom I once made a pink construction paper chart, back when I believed he and his brother must be counting the days—heck, counting the hours—until my return. But were they ever, really? Perhaps, deep down, I understood even then that the pink chart was more for me than for them. It was a retort to the voices in my head, the ones slinging guilt because I was leaving my babies for two weeks: *But I AM a good mom! See, I left this homemade chart, decorated with hearts and kisses and "Mommy loves you" messages and EVERYTHING!*

Clearly, we've outgrown the chart. Clearly, it's a good thing for a seventeen-year-old to be self-sufficient. But it is a strange bridge to cross, to have definitive proof that my firstborn, a boy once utterly dependent on me for food, for warmth, for everything . . . that I could skip town and not only would he not pine for me . . . he wouldn't even notice.

✳

I MEAN, YOU HAVE TO LAUGH," SAYS MY MOTHER, WHEN I JOG BACK TO HER KITCHEN AND TELL HER ABOUT THE CALL. "Here you are, literally writing a book about cherishing every last minute before the boys leave, every last night you're all under one roof. And here is James, so wrapped up in the demands of senior year, so ready to get on with his life, that he's oblivious as to whether you're sleeping in the same state as he is, forget under the same roof."

She's right. What can you do? I resolve to take my own advice, the part about how I control my own actions, only mine, no one else's. I control my decisions, and what I decided that day was— I'm done with missing my boys' soccer games.

If that sounds like a non sequitur, it circles back to the dilemma I laid out at the start, about school soccer kicking off at four p.m., the exact hour every afternoon that I go on air. I don't have the kind of job where you can knock off early and hope that no one notices. That Sunday morning call from James, asking me to move a car, came at the end of the summer before his senior year. I could not control whether he noticed my absence. But I could control whether I *was* absent, or whether I chose to show up this year. Soccer matters a great deal to my sons. My sons matter a great deal to me. And this was not exclusively about James's senior year. This was also the only season that the boys were likely to suit up in the same uniform, on the same field, at the same time. Both are strong players, but because of the two-year-and-two-month age gap, they'd never played on the same roster. For years, our family weekends had been an exercise in dividing and conquering, with Nick driving one kid to all his travel games and tournaments, and me driving the other, often dozens or hundreds of miles in the opposite direction. This was it: my chance to show up for both of them. Two birds, one stone.

I thought about the trade-offs involved in ceding the anchor chair for a long spell. They were not insignificant, but they were mine to make. So I asked to take six weeks of leave from the newsroom. I asked for the dates to overlap with peak high school soccer season. The plan was, I would write my butt off every day until three-thirty, then hit save, close my laptop, and race to the stadium to scream my head off at games.

It would be perfect.

And it was, some days.

My very first day of book leave was glorious. Early fall, crystalline blue skies, a hint of chill in the air but the sun still warm on your face. The words had flowed that morning. On the field, James took a few minutes to settle but when he did, he scored, and then he scored again. The second goal was courtesy of a cheeky flick off the back of his heel.

"Jeez, he made that look easy," whooped the dad of one of the younger boys, spinning around in the bleachers to give me a high five. It is surprising he could reach me, as I was levitating several feet off the ground with pride and love.

There were even better days. On his sixteenth birthday, Alexander scored in the last seconds of the game. His very first goal as a varsity player. Even the seniors stormed the field to congratulate him. You have never seen a boy with eyes so bright or a grin so wide. On the drive home, I teased him, "You know this is as good as life gets, right? A sweet goal, on your sweet sixteenth, in front of the whole school? You do know it's all downhill from here?"

The best day of all was an ordinary one, in a not particularly important game, early in the season. James and Alexander play the same position. This meant the downside of their being on the same team was that Alexander rarely got off the bench. As a senior, James started every game and finished most of them too; Alexander and many of the other younger players subbed in only if the score grew so lopsided in our favor that we were almost certain to win. When one player subs for another, they're supposed to do it fast, to minimize disruption. One player runs off, the other runs on, no drama, no breaking stride. When Alexander trotted onto the field to spell his brother that day, he held out his hand for a flying fist bump and kept moving. But for a sliver of a second, James stopped. He reached for Alexander's shoulder and squeezed it. A look passed from older brother to younger: *You got this.*

It was the smallest thing. No one else would have noticed. But I watched it and, like the Grinch, my heart grew three sizes that day.

NOT EVERY DAY WAS GREAT. I'll elide the details of the less glorious ones, out of respect for the boys' privacy. But there were days they played their hearts out and lost anyway. Days they came home bruised and discouraged. There were leg cramps and rain delays and a dislocated shoulder. There were days they limped off the field in tears.

I was there for all of it. Book leave slipped away, day by day. In the evenings, when dinner was finally cleared, the dishes washed, and the dog walked, I would settle on the sofa and try to write. And as often as not, the boys would interrupt.

"Mom, could you give this a quick read?" Alexander would ask, wanting a proofreader for his history paper on the rights of French women during the 1789 Revolution. James would ask to brainstorm on college essays. One night his task would be seven hundred words on why the University of Wisconsin was the only school for him. The next night, he needed to churn out an essay on why he belonged at Chicago, and only Chicago, *Crescat scientia*— Let knowledge grow! But the night after that? A thousand words on why he might die if he was not accepted at Tulane. You raise your child to tell the truth, but a few fibs are required to navigate the American college admissions process.

I did love these interruptions. Evenings like these are the whole point; they are the very subject of this book. It goes so fast. It is also true that writing—our heads bent together, debating whether a particular sentence demanded a semicolon or a hyphen—this was something we could share. I didn't have a lot to add to the family dinner conversations on sports or car repair. The boys had long ago concluded I had nothing useful to contribute on a great many subjects. But I knew how to edit and proofread, and I liked asking open questions, to help them figure out what it was they were trying to say. When their eyes lit up and they started madly banging away at their laptops, it made me feel like I might still have something to teach them.

As the evenings passed, though, with me happily googling the University of Wisconsin mascot (a badger) and the name of the student newspaper at Tulane (*The Hullabaloo*), my own chapters kept not getting written.

I was staring down a deadline. I knew how many words needed to get cranked out by the end of my six weeks of book leave, to have even a prayer of a chance of turning in this book on time. I was not close. Intervention was required. During the pandemic we had bought a beach house, an old barn on Nantucket that at some point over the years had been converted to an artist's studio and then to a private residence. I decided to go there, seal myself off for the last week of book leave, and do nothing but write. If you are reading this now, it worked. I wrote.

The price of going into hermit mode in order to write eighteen hours a day was that I missed a couple of games. The first was uneventful. Nick texted me from the second.

"0–0 so far," he reported.

"Go Bulldogs!" I replied. An hour and twenty-two minutes passed. Silence. I figured the game must be another slow one; otherwise, I would have heard an update.

"2–0," Nick texted at the end. And then: "James scored his best goal of the season."

"Really?" I asked later that night on the phone. "His best goal? Because remember, he had that great one in the game against—"

"No, this was much better. Definitely his best of the season. Incredible. He was so happy."

I scowled. This was *such* an Abu Simbel move.

ABU SIMBEL IS A MASSIVE TEMPLE COMPLEX, CARVED INTO ROCKS IN SOUTHERN EGYPT, DOWN NEAR THE BORDER WITH SUDAN. The Great Temple honors the pharaoh Ramesses II, and the Small Temple honors his senior wife, Queen Nefertari. Both were built in the thirteenth century BC.

Nick and I had visited exactly once, back in 2001, before the kids, back when we were practically kids ourselves. We had decided it would be a brilliant move to quit our jobs, sell our car and our flat in London, where we lived at the time, pack up everything we owned, and backpack around the world. This was in the days when you had to visit a physical travel agency to book such a thing. There were two competitor airline networks, with slightly different global routes and pricing schemes. As I recall, we chose the one that allowed you to stop in as many places as you liked, so long as the journey started and ended in the same country, and so long as you stuck to one global direction, either east or west around the globe. We chose west. We staggered out of the travel agency, loaded down with glossy brochures, and then spent a delicious week debating the merits of a stop in Brazil versus Peru (we chose Peru), China versus Japan (we chose both), Italy versus Greece (Greece). That old saw about how half the fun of taking a trip is planning it? Wrong. More like 95 percent.

Egypt, though. Egypt was a standout even on a multiweek odyssey of dream destinations. We signed up for a budget tour (we're talking seriously budget, to the extent that our Cairo hotel featured the unchanged bedsheets of the room's previous occupants, plus a jagged hole straight through the bathroom wall that afforded us charming, unobstructed views of the feet of pedestrians passing by on the street outside). But we got to do all the things that people travel to Egypt to do: we rode camels past the Great Pyramid of Giza, we visited King Tutankhamun's tomb, we scrambled around the massive columns of the ruins at Karnak. The final leg was a cruise down the Nile, sleeping in a cramped cabin on a mildewed but pleasant Egyptian boat incongruously named *The Amy*, as date palm trees and feluccas and boats heavy with other tourists floated past. The cruise finished in the southern city of Aswan. Here we were offered a choice: We could spend our last full day in Egypt exploring the city, before returning to Cairo and flying out. Or we could take an extremely expensive day trip—a round-trip flight to see the great pharaonic temples of Abu Simbel.

Now, I love a pharaonic temple as much as the next girl. But we had seen an awful lot of them in Egypt. Our tour guides prioritized ancient tombs and statues and mummies, which were of course the very sights that we had come to see. We'd had scant time, though, to glimpse daily life. The local rhythms and rituals. I wanted to go to the market in Aswan, wanted to bargain for fruit, to wander the streets and learn the Arabic words to order coffee in that town. The prospect of skipping that in order to rise before dawn to share a minivan to yet another airport to pack onto yet another plane with yet more tourists? Ugh.

But Nick was on a mission. "When are we ever going to get

back here? To the Egypt-Sudan border?" he asked, not unreasonably. "Don't you want to see it?"

"It costs a fortune," I protested. "For that price, we could order everything on the menu at the nicest restaurant in Cairo, and we'd still have change to spare. Plus, don't you want to see an actual town? See how people here live? We've been on trains and buses with other Western tourists this whole time. We've barely spoken to any Egyptians."

Why not split up for the day, you ask? Aha. Here we arrive at the heart of the matter. We could not split up for the day because I knew, with the certainty of someone who has been with their partner for a long time, that if he went and I didn't, he would return in a rapturous daze, stars in his eyes.

"That was the most incredible temple I have ever seen," he would report.

"Of course it was," I would reply long-sufferingly.

"Actually, it might be the most incredible thing I've ever seen, period. Mesmerizing. Life changing. Definitely the high point of this entire round-the-world trip. I so wish you'd been there."

He does not do this on purpose. But talk about inducing FOMO, fear of missing out. Our scrapbook from the trip contains eight photos of our day trip to Abu Simbel. A less gracious person might be tempted to note that they are wedged in alongside photos of many, many, many other temples in Egypt, from Cairo to the Valley of the Kings. A less gracious person might also note that the scrapbook contains precisely zero photos of me striking up a conversation with locals, zero of me at the Aswan market, zero of me bargaining for a pomegranate. . . . Zero, because these things never happened. Bygones. I will allow that the Abu Simbel temples were spectacular. In the photos, it's a very clear, cold day. Nick has captured me in front of the monumental main façade, wearing a baggy forest-green windbreaker, my eyes narrowed to slits. Against the sun? In irritation at the photographer? Hard to say. But after that, "Abu Simbel" became a running joke in our marriage, shorthand for Nick's unrepentant tendency to wax rhapsodic about any outing or event that I happen to miss.

It was such a classic Abu Simbel move for him to report that James had scored his best goal of his senior year at one of the tiny handful of games that I missed. So that night, from our barn in Nantucket, I checked the team video when it posted.

Goddammit.

It was true.

✳

I F I WAS NOT AS BEREFT AS YOU MIGHT EXPECT, IT WAS BECAUSE I HAD A CUNNING PLAN.

Yes, I had escaped to write for a week. Yes, I would miss two games. But I had deliberately timed my last day of book leave, a Friday, for the same day as the last regular season game. I organized my flights around this game as well. I would leave Nantucket first thing in the morning, land in DC by lunchtime, and have time to unpack and change before heading to the field. It would be exquisite: the symmetry of my last day away from the newsroom aligning with James's last non-playoff game of his high school career. I would arrive having written copiously, having for once, at last, figured out how to have it all and all at once.

At the beach house, the pages piled up. Do you know how much it is possible to get done, in a room in a house all by yourself, with no one to feed or worry about or answer to? With the candle burning low, then lower still, a blanket soft around your shoulders, the hours and the words unspooling, until you look up, realize it's well past midnight and you've forgotten to eat dinner? Virginia Woolf was definitely onto something.

It is true that there is nowhere on earth where I feel as alive as in a newsroom. But it might be in a room of my own, laboring away on the next essay or novel, that I feel the most content. The *yes baby yesss* moment of plucking just the right word from some cob-webbed corner of my brain. The satisfaction of surprising myself, when I set out to write about one thing and another story entirely spills out. Did I plan to write about Abu Simbel in this chapter? I did not. But it popped into my head, and if you had half as much fun reading it as I did writing it, then mission accomplished. How about the chapter on my father giving Alexander his first driving lesson? Did you enjoy that? No, you did not, because I deleted it. I was a thousand words down the rabbit hole of writing it before I realized it didn't belong in this book. Revising that now-deleted section, though, led me in a different, unexpected direction, which proved very useful indeed. This is how it works: Many days I have no idea what it is I'm trying to say until I force myself to hunker down at the keyboard and pound words onto the page. I have to dive into rabbit holes and get stuck, over and over, to figure out where I do want to go. Believe it or not, this process is *fun*.

And while I am all for stealing whatever morsels of time you can get to write—snatching ten minutes here, fifteen minutes there; they *do* add up—I will say that for me the good stuff can take time to marinate. It requires space and silence to make itself heard above the din. So, every once in a while, it helps to claim a room of one's own. You have to give yourself permission to close the door, and lock it, and then maybe jam the heaviest piece of furniture you own under the doorknob.

Some people are born better writers than others. But as far as I can tell, the main thing that distinguishes people who want to write a book from people who actually do so, is that they prioritize it. They decide to trust that they have something worth saying, and then they carve out and guard the time to say it.

Like many things, this is easier said than done.

So that solitary week in the beach house . . . it felt precious.

I HAD KNOWN WHEN I HATCHED MY PLAN FOR THIS SABBATICAL THAT I WOULD BE FLYING BACK TO A HUGE SOCCER GAME. It was against our archrival high school. They would have home field advantage. But it wasn't until the game where James scored the Abu Simbel goal that the rankings aligned to put the cup on the line. Suddenly first place in the league—the trophy for the regular season championship—was in play. Both my sons intimated that Friday would mark the most important game either of them had ever suited up for. Even from a distance, over phone calls and email, I could sense the tension building back at our house in Washington. I was excited too.

Then, on the Wednesday—some forty-eight hours before the big game was to take place—an email from the head coach arrived. The effect on me was like an incoming hand grenade. I reproduce the note, lightly edited, here:

Dear Soccer Families,

Friday's games have been moved to tomorrow due to anticipated weather conditions on Friday. The games will still begin at 4p.

JVII is now away at 4p.

I apologize for the inconvenience.

Go Bulldogs!

Coach

No. No no no no. Noooooooooo.

Long story short, I can't get there if they move the game up by a day. The same weather pattern that is causing them to shift the game forward in DC is already hitting where I am in New England. A nor'easter has knocked out power to parts of the island. Seventy-mile-per-hour wind gusts have been whipping branches against the roof and windows; just the night before, they had picked up the heavy wrought-iron patio furniture in our garden, spun and slammed it against the walls of the house, and left table and chairs and sun umbrella overturned in a heap. In the autumn on Nantucket, the only two ways on and off the island are by ferry—which is routinely canceled when the seas get too choppy—or by air, on a tiny ten-seater Cessna. The Cessnas don't fly in torrential rain or gale-force wind. I'm stuck.

Thursday—which is now game day—I wake up to yet more wind and reports of local flooding, power outages, and beached boats on Nantucket. The skies are overcast and skittish until a brief window when the sun appears, right around four p.m.

At that hour in Washington, the game is getting under way. No word yet. The minutes tick by.

"0–0 at halftime. James had a couple chances," Nick texts.

"There is no livestream so update me if something happens!!!" I text back.

In the second half, the archrival scores. Then we score. At the end of regular time, we are tied 1–1. But this game cannot end in a tie. Someone needs to win. The referee announces ten nail-biting minutes of golden goal overtime, meaning the moment that one team scores, it's over, and they take home the trophy.

A long time seems to pass.

Then Nick, who rarely swears, texts: "OMFG." *Oh My Fucking God.*

The next text: "James bullet header!!!!!!"

"2–1!!!!!"

"The league!!!!!!"

Texts and emails flood in from other parents.

"What a game, and what a goal by James!"

"Golden goal! In overtime! And with a header!"

"What a memory for your family. WooHoo!"

Alexander will later pronounce it the greatest moment in his years at the school. He has attended the school for seven years. I reach Nick on the sidelines. You can hear the celebration and mayhem behind him. "I am weeping," he tells me. "James will remember this his whole life."

I understand that this is not an Abu Simbel moment. Nick is not exaggerating. This is the real deal.

We hang up. I sit back on the sofa and I am weeping too, and they are tears of joy and tears of sadness, all mixed up. What I felt was so complicated. The overwhelming emotion, of course, was happiness for James. Also for Alexander, and for all their team-mates and their coaches, who had worked so hard all season, who never gave up. Nestled below that was frustration and fury, at myself. I should never have cut it so close; I should have found a way to get there; I should have strapped on flippers and swum from New England. Even deeper, down at the bottom, was something uglier. I suppose the right word for what I felt would be shame.

I had promised that this year would be different. I had promised that I would make a different choice, work be damned. I had promised these things, but here we were: James had scored the goal of his life, a goal he would never forget—and I had once again failed to show up.

CODA

———————•‣•———————

YOU *THINK* THE SOCCER SEASON IS OVER, BUT IT NEVER REALLY ENDS. I should have learned this by now. Many are the Saturday mornings when I've wandered into the kitchen and found Nick and the boys glued to the TV, watching soccer.

"Wait, I thought the season finished? Didn't we watch the Champions League final last week?"

"Yeah, but this is qualifiers for international play," Nick replies, as if this explains everything. No one else acknowledges me, no one says good morning, no one lifts their eyes from the screen. This would be tolerable for a finite period, but soccer is eternal. If England's Premier League isn't playing on a given weekend, the Scottish Premiership is. Or Spain's La Liga, or Serie A in Italy, or it's the run-up to the Copa América, or the Euros, or the World Cup, or . . . you get the picture.

As professional soccer goes, so goes high school. The never-ending nature of youth sports will be familiar to anyone who's ever played on a travel team, or raised a kid who plays travel. (The "off-season" is a highly flexible term, which some of our boys' coaches over the years have interpreted to include daily mandatory three-hour practices, plus a scrimmage or three on the weekends. Rest does not factor high on the list of coach priorities. Other priorities do not factor high on the list of coach priorities. Homework, anyone? Sleep?) I knew the boys would have a postseason, some sort of playoffs in late autumn. But I had been laboring under the impression that this would be an anticlimax, that surely nothing could top beating your archrival, in overtime, with a golden goal header, to take the regular season crown?

Silly me. Two more weeks of games appear to populate the team schedule, games that James informs me are in fact the most important of all. We may have won the league for the regular season, but now it's on to the league cup, and from there to the state championships. I, meanwhile, have exhausted my book leave. I'm back on air, back to navigating frantically busy days that build to the live broadcast, every day at four p.m. Having just asked for six weeks off, I couldn't countenance asking for more, couldn't imagine imposing on colleagues to cover for me any more than they already had.

It was time to call in reinforcements.

My mother's grasp of the game doesn't extend much beyond knowing you're supposed to put the ball in the goal, and you're not supposed to use your hands to do it. But she is the embodiment of a good sport, and when she learned there was a whole postseason to be played, she somehow guessed without our asking that I needed her, and that the boys did too. She could attend as both doting grandmother and as my surrogate; despite my absence, the boys would kick off every game knowing that a mom who loved them fiercely was in the stands. I had attended enough school sports games with her—dating back to my brother's glory days dominating T-ball, then high school and college baseball—to know how it would go.

"Get him!" she would yell. "Kick it! Get in there! Go Xander! Go Jamesie!"

It would be her mouth opening, her lips forming the words, but my voice would be hollering too. The generations keep watch over each other.

✳

WE'LL PASS LIGHTLY OVER THE RESULTS OF THE GAMES THAT MY MOTHER FLEW UP FOR. Suffice it to say that despite her exuberantly enthusiastic cheers, they were among the ones when the boys walked off the field in tears. After losing the league cup, James did not speak for a day or two. When he resumed communication, it was with ferocious focus and determination. James was in the middle of college applications. He had a full course load, including multiple AP classes. He had other extracurricular obligations. He had a girlfriend. But he was wholly focused on the DC State Athletic Association championship.

"So, which team looks toughest?" I asked, conversationally. "Who are you hoping you don't have to face?"

James shot me a withering look. "Why would you ask that? We'll face whoever we face. We'll beat whoever we need to beat. We're going to win."

Okaaaay then.

The day of the DC championship dawned cold, thirty-two degrees according to my weather app. We were the number 3 seed in the tournament. The team we were playing for the trophy was number 1.

The last time we had played them, back toward the beginning of the season, they had—as the *Washington Post* uncharitably put it—"trounced" us, winning by three goals. That was the bad news.

The good news? The final was scheduled for Sunday at six p.m. The weekend. Hallelujah. I can go.

James wakes up so nervous on the day of the final that he is incapable of eating. Alexander wisely stays out of his way. The hours pass slowly. Around five p.m., all the parents gather in the parking lot outside the stadium for a tailgate. A few of us have printed T-shirts, with "Go Bulldogs!" spelled out across the back. Nick orders pizzas; another family brings chicken wings; some rock star parent to whom I am deeply grateful produces a bubbling crockpot of chili, with cheese and toppings. We stress-eat everything in sight, more than compensating for our players' lost appetites.

At kickoff, both teams look cold and determined. We are playing under the bright lights of the big field at Catholic University, half an hour's drive from school, but a huge squad of students has made the trek to show support. It is still freezing. Shots go wide, our attackers swing and miss, neither side manages to string together more than a few passes. Halftime comes and goes. Twenty minutes into the second half, the score sits at 0–0. Then, suddenly, incredibly, one of our defenders heads the ball in. It's good. Score: 1–0. I whoop and clap and pull my scarf and hat tighter. The boys in the stands, immune in the way of teenage boys to cold, peel off their coats and shirts. Face paint in blue and white, the school colors, is passed around. Posters decorated with bulldogs are held high. But the other team looks dangerous, firing shot after shot on our goal, our goalie scampering to fend them off.

The score holds. All around me, parents have their eyes trained on the official countdown clock on the scoreboard. We'll take a 1–0 win. Let's just end this, please. The father in front of me is so tense he leaves his seat and climbs to the top row of the stadium where he commences pacing, visibly praying. Six minutes left to play. Five. Four. *Run down the clock run down the clock run down the clock.*

And then: OMFG.

Goal.

James.

The official school athletic account, which is live-tweeting the game, posts the following: "James Boyle header! 2–0 Dogs! 3:00 left."

The parents around me go berserk. The shirtless hordes in the student section go berserk, jumping up and down as one, arms tight around each other's waists, chanting, pressing closer to the barrier.

"Fans, do NOT storm the field," the announcer intones from the press box. "I repeat, do NOT storm the field."

Two minutes.

One.

And then it's over. Final score: 2–0.

Victory laps are taken. Both teams line up to shake hands. They were a worthy adversary; this could easily have tipped the other way. The trophy is presented. The headmaster jumps the barrier to pose for photographs with the team captains. From the field, James blows me a kiss.

Afterward, he jogs to the sidelines. He greets his lacrosse coach first, a bear of a man who didn't need to show up for a different sport but who has attended every game, even the away games, and who cheered louder than any of us.

"I swear you were the only one I could hear, Coach," James tells him. "Thank you for coming."

Then he turns to me. I stand on my tiptoes to hug him. "So proud of you," I whisper.

"Love you, Mom," he whispers back. And then he moves on, high-fiving his way down a line of well-wishers.

If this were fiction, my editor would nix it. Too improbable a happy ending, too sugary, too Hallmark Channel. Totally. Agreed.

But it happened as it happened. They played. They won. James scored. I was there.

It took another mother, my own, to understand how much it mattered. She had returned to Atlanta by then, so I called her from the car on the drive home. I told her about the win, about James's goal, how beautiful the trophy was, how he had hoisted it high over his head, how happy all the boys looked, how the moms and quite a few of the dads had cried. My mother listened to the full account. Her first words weren't to ask for more details about the game or even to say how proud she was of James and Alexander. They were for me, her daughter—her own firstborn.

"Oh, Sunshine," she said, which is what she calls me when she's happy. "How wonderful. And you got to see it! I'm so glad for you. I'm so glad that you were there."

WHAT WE PASS ON

M‍Y FATHER'S NAME WAS JAMES.
His father's name was also James, and his grandfather's before that.

Nick's father's name is James. His father was also James, and his grandfather before that. There are in fact so many people named James on Nick's side of the family that one of his cousins in Glasgow good-naturedly puts up with being known as Medium-Sized James, to distinguish him from, among others, Big James and Wee James. Wee James is my son James, and if we're going purely by height, he is now technically the biggest James of all.

Nick is . . . Nick. Short for Nicholas. But his middle name is—wait for it, you'll never, ever guess—James. Does it go without saying that when I was pregnant with our first and we learned it was a boy, there was a *strong* contender for what to call him? We would christen him James, honor both our fathers and indeed nearly every male on both sides of the family in one fell swoop, and be done with it. For the next kid, we would be free to choose whatever name we liked.

Somehow, though, Nick kept working in more of his family names. We gave our James the middle name Cameron, which is also from Nick's side of the family. Nick's great-aunts and great-uncles are all Camerons; on formal occasions, Nick and his brothers wear kilts stitched from the family Cameron tartan. That seemed a lovely thing to hold on to. But it means that all three of my firstborn child's names—first, middle, and last—are passed down from his father. With Alexander, it's two out of three. He also carries his father's surname, and we gave him "Nicholas" as his middle name. "Alexander" is the only outlier, the only nonfamily name; we just liked it.

The women in the family are less methodical about all this. Surnames are relegated at marriage; I'm the only one on either side to have kept my maiden name. And there are no dominant female names passed down generation after generation. The only one that comes close is *Louise*. I share my middle name with my mother, and my full name with her mother, Mary Louise Humphries. I might have named my daughter Mary Louise, if I'd had one, which I didn't, and after the complications with Alexander's delivery, we were told it would not be wise to try again. This means that unlike my husband—whose first, middle, and last names will live on through our children—no one is named for me. I had never given this much thought, had not realized it bugged me. And then one day, through a most unlikely way, I learned that it is not true.

Someone *is* named for me. She lives in Kansas City, Missouri, and she is a chicken.

✳

I DON'T KNOW THAT THERE'S A TYPICAL, WELL-TRODDEN PATH TO LEARNING THAT YOU HAVE A LIVING, CLUCKING POULTRY NAMESAKE, BUT I WILL SAY THAT I WAS NOT EXPECTING TO ACQUIRE THIS

INFORMATION WHILE REPORTING ABOUT A MIGRANT CRISIS UNFOLD-
ING AT THE BELARUS-POLAND BORDER. In the autumn of 2021, thousands of people fleeing the Middle East and beyond were caught
in a no-man's-land of tents and desperation, sleeping in the frigid
forest, with armed and unyielding Polish security forces lined up
on one side, and equally armed and unyielding Belarussian forces
lined up on the other. Children were dying. It was a desperate
situation. We had just interviewed a journalist with an eyewitness
account, and I tweeted out the interview, hoping to call attention
to the migrants' plight. You tweet something like that and you
expect the first people who engage to be other journalists, human
rights groups, or government officials. But the first reply, posted
exactly two minutes after my initial tweet, was this:

"Just so you know, I named a chicken after you, fine lady journalist."

A chicken? I thought.

"A chicken?" I typed back. "Might you send a photo?"

Minutes later, one appeared. God, she was gorgeous.

Rich russet feathers. Flecks of white in her tail. Healthy. You
could tell that she was sassy, the kind of hen who would brook no
nonsense.

The owner and I swapped a few more messages. I learned that
my chicken's full name was Mary Louise Klucky, and that she
shared a coop with Ruth Bader Ginsbird and Sonia Sotomayover-
easy. I have no idea what I did to deserve accommodation with
Supreme Court justices. I do know that I blush to admit I was so
touched by it. That I felt kinship with a random chicken in Kansas City, just because she bore my name.

I honestly don't remember why I didn't push to bestow a name
from my side on at least one of the boys. I could have insisted on
"Kelly" as a middle name. Or "Louis." Or "Christopher," for
my brother. I do love family names. The weight and tradition of

them, the sense of belonging that they confer, the way they wrap around generations, sometimes shortened or spelled differently, sometimes crossing gender or disappearing for decades, until a tiny newborn pops out and the parents decide to christen her with the name of some formidable, long-dead and much-missed great-aunt.

It's not like Nick would have fought me. I think part of what factored into my passivity was that when I had my kids, I wasn't old enough yet to grasp that time was not infinite, that I would not be around forever, that my name would die with me unless I did something proactive about it. A second contributing factor is the unfortunate but true fact that after we'd exhausted "James," my side of the family didn't offer up a lot of boy names to work with. I adored my mother's father and her brother—my grandfather and my only uncle—and would have loved to honor them. But their names were Verlin Ralph and Verlin Ralph Junior. With sincere respect for all the wonderful gentlemen out there named Verlin and Ralph, I was okay with retiring these names to the twentieth century.

Looking at her photo again, I wondered but did not inquire as to whether Mary Louise Klucky was being raised for her eggs or for her meat. The former seemed more likely, given that they'd bothered to name her. But was there some inherent difference? With cows, some are kept to produce milk and others to be sold as beef. Were some chickens raised to produce eggs and others, an entirely different category from birth, raised to be sold, plucked and trussed, before eventually landing on the rotisserie spit at my grocery store? I'm embarrassed to confess I wasn't sure.

I tried to think who would know such a thing off the top of their head. The answer came immediately: Dad.

✳

MY FATHER, JAMES "JIM" KELLY, POSSESSED AN ENCYCLOPEDIC KNOWLEDGE OF A DIZZYING NUMBER OF SUBJECTS. Yes, yes, I know—many little girls believe their daddy knows everything about everything. But mine really did. He was voraciously curious about the most random things, and he read constantly. Wander into a room in our house, especially in Dad's later years, when he'd slowed down and when he could finally afford to hire help to tend to most of the yard work and the gutter sweeping and the driveway-crack repairing and the paint touch-ups and the myriad other, never-ending handyman chores, and chances were you would find him, reading glasses slipping down his nose, engrossed in either the daily newspaper or a nonfiction tome. History, biography, economics, law, science, foreign affairs—he read everything. And unlike me, he seemed to retain every word.

The only thing my father loved more than acquiring knowledge was sharing it, and usually my brother, C.J., and I were the nearest ~~victims~~—er, beneficiaries.

Dad never lived down the forced family outings to the Etowah Indian Mounds. The mounds form a historic site in Bartow County, Georgia, once home, at various points from AD 1000 to AD 1550, to several thousand members of the Muscogee (Creek) and Cherokee peoples. Both tribes still hold the land to be sacred. Dad had an admirable intention: to teach us respect for the history. He wanted us to understand whose land this was, how these people lived, what had happened to them. I have no doubt that it's possible to have an interesting, educational family day trip to the site. I have no doubt that the site is worthy of study and reflection. But back when we were kids, we were not yet capable of absorbing the full freight of the history that Dad was trying to impart. Our shared ~~misery~~ experience was a car sickness–inducing drive, bickering in the sweltering back seat of the family car, which in those years was a banana-yellow Buick station wagon of spaceship-sized proportions.

After what seemed an eternity, we would pull into the parking lot, unstick ourselves from the damp seats, and glimpse . . . modest mounds of grass. Truly, from a six-year-old's perspective, that was seemingly it. That was all there was to see. Six earthen mounds, ranging from a few feet to a few dozen feet high. Dad would summit one and proceed to lecture for an hour, maybe more, about the artifacts that had been found nearby, from arrowheads and effigies to seashells and copper ornaments.

We made this excursion several times, until finally Mom put her foot down.

My father persisted. For years. He believed that we would all come to revere the Etowah Indian Mounds as he did, if only he could talk long enough to spark our enthusiasm.

This was not an isolated incident.

I was not in the car on the memorable day that my parents were driving my brother and one of his buddies to a movie and the buddy, innocent as a lamb, piped up from the back seat: "Mr. Kelly, what's a Mormon?" Neither Mom nor C.J. can remember what prompted the question. They do remember exchanging alarmed looks and trying to change the subject. Too late. The entire history of the Church of Jesus Christ of Latter-day Saints was unlocked. My mother and brother swear an hour passed before Dad paused for breath and the boys were allowed to ~~flee~~ get out of the car.

I *was* there, unfortunately, for my infamous high school history paper on the Huguenots. The Huguenots were Protestants in France in the sixteenth and seventeenth centuries. They followed the teachings of John Calvin and suffered severe persecution for their faith. Would you like to know more about the Huguenots? Like, a LOT more? Jim Kelly was your guy. It's a mystery how he knew so much, impressive even by his standards. The evening that I mentioned the topic of my paper at dinner, I had already squirreled away every relevant encyclopedia in the house. They were spread on the floor around my desk in my bedroom, along with library books and our class textbook. And remember, this was the late 1980s, before you could look stuff up on your phone or computer. There was no way Dad could have researched the Huguenots after we finished dinner, and if he'd ever taken a French history class, it would have been decades previously. But that same night, as I worked, trying to structure my outline, Dad eased himself into an armchair beside me, a look of eager concentration on his face.

"Yes?"

"Have you figured out yet how you're going to handle the Edict of Nantes, and everything Louis XIV did after?"

And he was off.

I got an A on the paper. I remember almost nothing else about it; I recall none of the historical details; I had to pull out my phone just now and look up that I had the right King Louis, before typing the sentence above.

Dad would have known the answer to my question about chickens. He would have explained everything patiently, and once he'd dispensed with that he would have instructed me on the finer points of building a henhouse, and how to protect the hens from foxes. He would then have shared thoughts on the economics of egg farming, how the biggest cost is labor. And finally, warming to his subject, he might have made sure I knew where to find the best barbecue chicken joint in every town in northern Georgia.

✳

I INHERITED MY FATHER'S TENDENCY TO DRONE ON. To this day, I'll be talking merrily away about something or other and C.J. will catch my eye and whisper, too low for others at the table to hear:

Huguenots. I'll look around and realize everyone's eyes are rolling back in their heads.

Among the other things I inherited: my father's last name. Our branch of Kellys came over from Ireland in the nineteenth century and took jobs as cops and housecleaners, mostly in Philadelphia, a few in Boston. Perhaps it was all these industrious Kellys who passed on to my father, who then passed on to me, a capacity for and an inclination toward hard work.

What else? My father's big, broad feet. His big, broad hands. His love for the solitary, knee-sabotaging sport of running.

All this, and a killer cocktail recipe.

My father was not a drinker. But he loved learning about wine, which one to pair with which food, to elevate your meal from tasty to sublime. He loved a stein of crisp, golden German pilsner—a legacy from his years of service in the U.S. Army, stationed in Bavaria. He cared about appearances. The correct glass was absolutely required; this was not a man who chugged beer from a can. And he loved a good cocktail. He was going to drink only one, so it needed to count. Dad lacked patience for syrups and fruity add-ons and frou-frou garnishes. His rule for cocktails was that they should be three things: simple, cold, and strong.

Dad's drink was a Manhattan. He was true to it his whole life. His preferred spirits evolved over the years, as he tried new things and was able to buy better-quality booze. Although I had watched him make one many times, I'd never paid much attention to how he was doing it. So one day toward the end, when he was no longer drinking or even eating much of anything, I dragged a chair up to my parents' kitchen counter, got him settled, and asked him to teach me.

We went through it step-by-step. The chilling, the measuring, the shaking. Cocktails are like travel, in that so much of the pleasure lies in the anticipation. By this point Dad had been so sick for so long, but in that moment together it felt briefly like all was right in the world: him holding forth, explaining in somewhat greater detail than necessary how to mix a drink. Me listening, dutifully completing each step as instructed, hiding a smile, mouthing silently to myself, *Huguenots*.

I told him that I would write it all down. I told him that one day I would teach the boys, his grandsons, how to make his drink. That it would be among the things they inherited from him. Meantime, I think he'd be tickled to know his recipe—another thing that bears his name—was out there in the world.

Here it is:

PAPA JIM'S MANHATTAN

- 2 ounces Redemption Rye whiskey (acceptable, slightly sweeter alternative: 2 ounces Woodford Reserve bourbon whiskey)
- 1 ounce Antica Formula vermouth
- Angostura bitters, waved in the general direction

Combine with ice in a cocktail shaker, shake until the outside of the shaker turns frosty. (Yes, my father was aware that some purists insist on stirring instead of shaking. He wished them well and trusted that one day they might see the error of their ways.)

Strain into a chilled martini glass.

If you must, drop in a Luxardo cherry.

Cheers, Dad. I miss you so.

WE'RE NEARLY HOME

I WANT TO WRITE MORE ABOUT MY FATHER HERE. I want to write about how he taught me to be a runner, about how I see him in my sons—but find that I cannot. The words won't come. I have tried for days. I am trying now.

Nine months since he died, and the fog of grief has lifted. What remains is like a knife, sheathed until I least expect it, then slicing sharply, triggered by the oddest things. I expected to feel sad on his birthday, what would have been his seventh-fifth, and I did. I expected to feel sad on my first Father's Day without him. And the first Thanksgiving, when we all sat down to turkey and my brother, my husband, and I stared at each other, a little lost as to how the meal might begin without Dad presiding, delivering his traditional rambling grace, which always opened with thanking the Lord for the blessings He had bestowed upon us, and always ended with thanks to the members of our nation's armed forces for their service.

I was braced for all of these firsts.

What I was not braced for was the knife darting out, stabbing, and twisting, on a quotidian errand like getting my hair cut. There was no reason to be thinking of Dad. He'd never visited my salon, could not have told you its name or where it was. I had been a stranger myself of late, neglecting my hair. It was the pandemic, I never went anywhere, everything was awful, what was the point? My ends were split and frizzy, and strands of silver were poking up amid the blond.

When I finally made an appointment and settled into the swivel chair of my longtime hairdresser—the same one who had wisely overruled my desire to go brunette—I announced that I was tired of long hair. It was time to chop off at least eight inches. He raised his eyebrows at this but nodded, *okay*. Also, I continued, I was ready to go gray. Enough with the golden highlights, enough with artfully disguising my roots.

"Really?" He looked skeptical.

Oh yes, I informed him. Definitely. Who was I fooling? After all, I was the mother of a son who had just turned eighteen, a child who was now officially a man. I had friends who had allowed their hair to grow in gray and loved it. I was fine with looking my age. I was done with dye jobs, with the hassle and the maintenance, I told him. *I am already a woman who no one wolf-whistles at anymore*, I thought but did not say.

He shook his head. "Not yet. I think you will not like it."

"I'll like it."

"No," he said more firmly. "Your hair is still mostly blond. We'll know when you are ready."

I was about to argue with him.

But then he was running his fingers through my hair, tugging it this way and that, talking through options. The way his hands cupped my scalp was familiar and gentle. This man, whom I had never seen outside of the salon, had been running his fingers through my hair and talking me out of bad ideas for more than a dozen years. His voice was deep. His hands were warm. His eyes were kind. And all of a sudden, I came undone.

I had to sit for a long moment, tears flooding down my cheeks, before I figured out why. I was crying because my dad had seen this hair. The day he died I had sat beside him in bed, reading to him and telling him stories, not sure if he could hear me. He was struggling to breathe, making a crackling, wheezing sound; I had never heard a death rattle before. I had leaned down to kiss him and when I did, my hair had brushed his cheek. *This* hair. The last time my father looked at me, he had seen this hair. He would never see the new haircut or any of the ones that followed. He would never know me with gray hair. Life was carrying on, and I would grow old, and Dad was not here.

I did not attempt to explain all this to my hairdresser. I didn't fully understand it myself. I sniffled, said I was sorry, that it was nothing, that I was having a sad day. He brought me a mug of ginger tea and the new issue of *People* magazine. We agreed that I was too young to have gray hair. We would know when it was time, and when it was, my silver mane would look divine. In the meantime, he proceeded to apply the same shade of highlights that he always does. He sheared off eight inches and feathered the front and blew it dry smooth, with a little flip. I felt so much better by the time I paid and left. I had forgotten what it was to feel pretty.

I want to write about my father and how he taught me to be a runner, about how I see him in my sons. I can't. Not yet. The tears come easily but the words do not. So let's hit pause on this chapter and come back to it another day, shall we?

LETTING THE SILENCE PLAY OUT

———◆◆———

A THING I HAVE NOT MENTIONED: I AM DEAF, OR CLOSE TO IT, WITH HEARING LOSS IN THE SEVERE-TO-PROFOUND RANGE AT HIGH FREQUENCIES. I anchor a national news broadcast every evening wearing hearing aids, both ears. This presents its challenges. My job requires me to ask people questions and then listen—really *listen*—to the answers. How can I do that if I cannot hear you?

Our main studios at NPR headquarters are not a problem. Actually, they're a dream: professionally soundproofed, zero background noise, equipped with top-of-the-line Sony headphones that I can crank as loud as I need during interviews. You would in fact struggle to conjure up a more hospitable work environment for a person with a hearing impairment.

Trouble is, I'm not always in our studios. Take the pandemic. Along with just about everyone else who held an office job, NPR staffers pivoted overnight to working from home. Those beautiful, soundproofed, you-can-hear-a-pin-drop studios went dark. My cohosts all nimbly jumped to conducting interviews from their bedrooms and basements, mostly via Zoom, dogs and kids howling in the background. They would speak into broadcast-quality mics, recording their end of the conversation, while a team of editors and producers listened in from their own homes, on mute, but able to monitor audio levels and record the guest's answers. This setup is obviously not ideal. And if you wear hearing aids, it just plain doesn't work. I had to ask for accommodations. These included routing almost all my interviews through the master operations desk at headquarters, despite the fact that neither my guest nor I were there. It was more hassle for our producers and engineers, and I felt bad about that, but it had the distinct benefit of allowing me to hear what the person I was interviewing was saying.

Then there is what is hands down my favorite part of my job: escaping Washington entirely, to report from the field. So many times, on the street or in a crowd, I've had to ask someone I'm interviewing, "Can you speak up please? Can you repeat that? A little louder?"

I have a particularly vivid memory from 2017, of standing on Tverskaya, Moscow's main drag, with anti-Kremlin protests swirling around me. The protesters were chanting, "Putin Vor! Putin Vor!" ("Putin is a thief! Putin is a thief!") Security forces wearing body armor and wielding batons were wading into the fray, either leading protesters away or—if they wouldn't come voluntarily—knocking them to the ground and dragging them off to waiting vans. Rubber bullets were flying. Helicopters circled low. The noise was indescribable.

NPR security protocols stipulate that you don't cover a protest alone if you can possibly avoid it, especially one that is turning violent. I had arranged to meet Sergei Sotnikov, our Moscow bureau's indefatigable producer, on Pushkin Square, the epicenter of the protest. We would work together to file for *Morning Edition*, the program on air at that hour, plus newscasts and NPR's social media platforms. But we were arriving at the square from different directions and found ourselves marooned on opposite sides of a security cordon. He texted me over and over from our agreed meeting point, trying to coach me through how to reach him. No luck. The streets were sealed, ditto the back alleys, ditto the underground entrances to the Moscow metro tunnels that might have popped me up on his side of the square. This meant I was stranded without an interpreter, unable to interview Russian speakers. It also meant I was stranded without all of the broadcasting gear in Sergei's backpack. I'd brought a backup kit in my own bag, including a Comrex—a sleek black audio modem about half the size of a cereal box that we use for remote broadcasts. It had performed beautifully when I tested it at the bureau just hours before. Now, with me swearing at it, squatting behind a trash bin and trying to avoid getting kicked or arrested as the melee around me rolled on, the Comrex resolutely refused to connect.

I was left with only a cell phone, on my own, updating *Morning Edition* live every hour. For any other reporter, this arrangement would have been manageable. But this was back before my hearing aids featured Bluetooth and the ability to pipe calls directly into my ears. To speak on my phone, I had to use wired earbuds, which meant removing my hearing aids; there isn't room in your ears for both at the same time. The volume on my cell would go only so high, and without my hearing aids to amplify, it wasn't nearly high enough.

My friend David Greene was anchoring that morning. As a former Moscow correspondent, he knew the Russia story inside out. That was the upside of his being on duty that day. The downside was that neither David nor I are known for sticking to a script. Ad-libbing and being quick on your feet are what make live broadcasting fun. Normally I love the adrenaline of spontaneous back-and-forth, of never knowing what my colleague might say or where the conversation might go next. But that day I remember texting him something to the effect of "Friend, may I beg you please for once to ask me the questions exactly as I've scripted them here? And in this exact order?"

Live hit after live hit, I struggled. I could just about make out when David said my name, and when he paused, and then I would start talking. By the end, closing in on seven straight hours of broadcasting, David was wandering off script, throwing in asides and follow-ups, embroidering my account with added context and reporting of his own. He couldn't help himself. I couldn't blame him. It was exactly what a seasoned anchor should do. So I screwed my eyes shut in concentration, jammed the earbuds even deeper into my ear canals, and prayed. When I couldn't tell whether it was my turn to talk, I would listen for the up inflection in his voice, and then the pause, and it was enough.

THE THING ABOUT GOING DEAF IS YOU DON'T REALIZE IT'S HAPPENING. It's impossible to pinpoint when everyone around you begins to mumble, when you cease hearing your own footsteps clicking down a hall.

Like many people who require hearing aids in order to function, I can still pass the perfunctory test at my annual physical, the one where you're told to raise your hand when you hear the beep. Most of the time I can hear the damn beep. I do need help with volume, but the main thing I can't do is recognize words and distinguish consonants. Did you just offer me a *cub* of coffee? A *cut* of coffee? I can't hear the difference, but I'll go out on a limb here and guess that you asked if I'd like . . . a *cup*.

You can fake it for a long time, nodding and smiling agreeably, even as you have no idea what's being said. You can blame it on a cold that's stuffed up your ears, or on the clatter of a noisy café.

Or on moving to a foreign country—which I did, in 2013, and then spent a full year insisting that the reason I couldn't understand anyone was that my Italian needed work. But I had long known what likely loomed in my future. Yes, I'd spent time on aircraft carriers, and aboard noisy helicopters in noisy war zones. Yes, I had probably done some damage by cranking those Sony headphones in the studio too loud, for years. But the most likely explanation for my hearing loss is genetics. My grandmother was profoundly hard of hearing, and so was her son, my father. Yet another thing I inherited from Jim Kelly.

For me, the breaking point was a book tour during which I was crippled, at event after event, by not being able to hear the audience questions. This was 2014. The tour was to promote my first novel. I remember one event in particular, when a woman rose and asked a question that had the audience in stitches. I squirmed, laughed along, and responded with what was surely a non sequitur, as I'd barely caught a word of what she'd said. In the taxi home, my cheeks still crimson with embarrassment, I thought: *Enough.*

Still, none of this prepared me for sitting in an audiologist's office, at the age of forty-three, and being told that I suffered severe hearing loss in both ears. How severe? In one test, the audiologist stood across the room from me, said a word out loud in a normal voice, and asked me to repeat what I had heard.

"Void," he said.

"Void," I repeated.

"Ditch," he said.

"Ditch."

Out of twenty words, I got sixteen. "Not perfect, but hardly *severe*," I sniffed.

But for the next round, he performed the test holding a sheet of paper before his face, so that I could not see his lips.

"*Mumble*," he said.

LETTING THE SILENCE PLAY OUT ✦ 125

"Repeat that one?"

"*Mumble mumble,*" he said.

"Er . . . shoelace?"

"Nope. *Mumbledy mumble.*"

And so it went. This time, out of twenty words, I got six. When I could not see a person's lips moving, I missed 70 percent of what they said. *Seventy percent.* Since then, my hearing has worsened, a little every year. Doctors can't say whether it will eventually stabilize. Nor can they tell me when exactly this began. Did I hear normally in my twenties and thirties? I thought I did, but who knows?

My first day with hearing aids, I went about my routines with a sense of wonder. It was astonishing to rediscover that pop songs have words, words that I could hear and sing along to. "Have been bopping to an '80s dance mix all morning," I posted on Facebook. "I challenge anyone to deny Debbie Gibson was a genius ahead of her time." (To which came the inevitable reply: "You need to get your hearing checked.")

By day two, I was on sensory overload. "Starbucks is the noisiest place in the world," I posted. "Who knew frothing milk made such a racket?" That afternoon I jogged five miles along the trails in Rock Creek Park. For the first time in years, I didn't jump in fright every time cyclists whizzed past, because I could hear them coming.

My keenest memory, though, of that first summer with hearing aids is of driving our car one afternoon, the boys strapped in the back seat, chattering away. I had picked them up from summer camp, and they were giggling, talking about something silly that had happened that day. It hit me like a bolt of lightning: They must have been doing this all along. They must have been chattering away *for years.* I listened, a lump growing in my throat. Partly for joy that I could hear them now. And partly at the realization of all that I had missed.

✳

THE MOST OBVIOUS INSIGHT I CAN SHARE ABOUT TRYING TO TALK WITH TEENAGERS WHEN YOU ARE DEAF IS THAT IT'S HARDER TO HEAR THEM. And it's . . . already so hard. You're already talking past each other, failing to communicate on things large and small.

Picture James and me in the kitchen. He's standing at the sink, telling me something, but I'm not wearing my hearing aids, and I can't make out what he's saying. I do try to wear them when I'm likely to encounter other humans. This is for me, obviously, so that I can hear, but also out of respect for the rest of you, so I don't have to ask you to repeat yourselves a million times.

Then there's the fact that hearing aids help more if you wear them consistently, every day. Your brain forgets how to understand sounds if it goes without hearing them for a while. I suspect this is what happened to me during the years that I went undiagnosed. It takes time for the brain to adjust, to relearn the pathways it once knew. I'm not sure you ever recover all that was lost. Today I don't hear perfectly even wearing hearing aids; I still can't watch TV without the subtitles on.

But there is also the fact that hearing aids are uncomfortable. You get used to them, and minor discomfort seems a minor price to pay. But you're still sticking a metal speaker deep inside your ear, connected via a plastic-coated wire to a larger gizmo parked on the back of your ear, which contains the microphone, an amplifier, and a battery. Many people are also fitted with stabilizers, curving pieces of plastic that nestle inside your outer ear to keep the whole contraption from coming loose. Ever worn a ponytail? A way-too-tight ponytail that you didn't realize was annoying you until you get home at the end of the day, pull loose the elastic band, and shake free your hair? Bliss. Blessed release. Heaven. This is what it feels like to remove hearing aids at night.

And this is why, if you were to peek into our kitchen on a typical weekend morning, you would likely find me padding around in my pajamas, wearing my glasses, teeth not yet brushed, and hearing aids not yet in. If they're working as they should, hearing aids jolt the world into focus. Everything crisp and loud and sharp. When you're still in slippers, waiting for the coffee to brew, it can feel a little much. Donning them first thing on a lazy Saturday feels about as appealing as rolling straight out of bed and straight into Spanx, full makeup, and an aggressive power suit. No, thank you.

But while I'm rustling around, fuzzy with sleep, James will appear. I haven't heard him come down the back stairs, of course. Haven't realized he's there until I turn around and see he's at the sink, filling a glass of water. His lips are moving and God knows how long he's been talking.

"Good morning, sweet boy. What was that? Say it again?"

So he says it again, but he's mumbling, truly he is. I catch every fourth word, and my mind is racing to fill in what other words must belong in those gaps, trying to figure out if he's sharing some Deep Important Thought, or merely asking if there's toast. He glances up, searches my face, and sees that I don't understand.

"Never *mind*, Mom. Forget it." He clomps away. At these moments, I know we both want to scream (and in my case, it would help immensely if James would indeed just let rip). I follow him to the next room. Ask him to stop. Try to plant myself in front of him where I can see and read his lips. But by now he's annoyed, shaking his head, shaking me off.

"It doesn't matter anyway. I'll ask Dad."

I can stand there pleading, but the moment has passed. I'll never know what was on his mind.

✳

YOU WOULD THINK I WOULD BE GOOD AT GETTING MY FAMILY TO TALK. It's what I do for a living, for God's sake. When you're interviewing someone who clams up, who is reluctant for whatever reason to say much, or to venture beyond their prepared talking points, two of the most useful questions are "Why?" and "Give me an example?" Politicians in particular are great at throwing around all kinds of sweeping, abstract statements. But encourage them with a simple "Why?" and you may elicit an answer you can wrap your arms around. It's fun; sometimes you realize you're listening to someone figuring out in real time what they think about an issue.

Another technique I recommend to beginning journalists is to embrace silence. Don't rush to fill the space. Let the silence play out. This takes practice and guts, to ask a question and then wait. Do you know how long three seconds of dead air can feel? Five? Ten? It's excruciatingly uncomfortable. But if you steel yourself, the person you're interviewing may eventually answer—and this answer may prove the most genuine, revealing, and memorable of the entire interview.

Good luck trying this on teenagers, though. They have no problem letting the silence play out. Ask them a question they don't want to answer and they'll sit on it and keep you waiting . . . forever.

Me: Why did you miss curfew last night?

Teenage son: (*silence*)

Me: And what time did your brother come home? Because we didn't see him come in either.

Teenage son: (*yet more silence*)

Me: Also, did you eat the chocolate cake in the fridge? The piece I'd hidden in the back with a note taped on it, "Mom is saving—Do NOT eat"?

Teenage son: (*unbending, impenetrable silence*)

After each attempt, five seconds will pass. Ten. Twenty. At a certain point I've lost interest; I'm just looking for a face-saving way to make this conversation end. I'll hear myself start to babble, "Well, if it happens again . . ." My children have a 100 percent track record of getting me to cave first.

Sometimes I suspect they're playing the long game, betting that as the years pass I'll lose my marbles as well as my hearing. That eventually, if they sit silently for long enough, I'll forget what question I was asking in the first place.

✳

*W*HY SHOULD THINGS BE EASY WHEN THEY CAN BE DIFFICULT? I am told this is an old Bulgarian saying. I learned it from a Bulgarian friend and colleague, Monika Evstatieva. Mo was born in the capital, Sofia, in the twilight years of the Warsaw Pact, and it sounds better when she says it, in an exasperated growl, *Zashto da e lesno, kato moje da e trudno.* She tells me the phrase captures both the hardship of life under Ottoman and then Communist rule, and the bleak humor that helped people survive.

The occasion for her teaching it to me was a reporting trip to Russia—a different one, the year after the protests during which Sergei and I got marooned on opposite sides of Pushkin Square. Mo and I were there to cover the presidential election of 2018, or as many of the people we met viewed it, the corrupt, devoid-of-suspense, rigged coronation of Vladimir Putin for a fourth term.

Some reporting trips are better than others. More productive, richer. Before a big one, you prep for weeks, lining up interviews and scouting stories. This advance legwork is critical. But as with much in life, how it all shakes out often comes down to luck, and on this particular trip, we were exceptionally lucky. *Everyone* wanted to talk. We were drowning in amazing interviews. It was March and bitterly cold, snow blanketing the streets, and we would step out the front door of our hotel and stumble upon three stories we wanted to do before we could cross the street and find breakfast.

We interviewed the leader of an independent election watchdog group, who showed me footage he'd obtained of ballot boxes being tampered with during legislative elections two years before.

"Behold!" he crowed, as we watched. "They stuff it, stuff it, stuff it."

We interviewed the sweet-looking grandmother in charge of Moscow voting station number 1096. She sat us down at her dining room table and delivered a master class on speaking truth to power, shaking her fists in the air, making it plain that anyone who tried to stuff a ballot box in her precinct would have to do so over her dead body.

"I think the way you combat fraud and you fight lies is by speaking up," she said, and she quoted a passage from Solzhenitsyn. My fingers cramped and ached, I was writing so furiously in my reporter's notebook, trying to get down every word.

We met a pro-Putin youth leader at his office, a Brooklyn-style loft that shared an alley with an old bread factory. He told me he liked Putin, among other reasons, because these days he had to fight to find a parking space at his apartment building.

And . . . this was a good development? I asked, puzzled.

Sure, he replied. Because under Putin, people had more money. They could get loans. They could afford a car.

For a break from the politics, we went to meet a Russian chef who was busy reinventing his country's cuisine. The idea was to erase the memory of gross, gray Soviet meals and reintroduce the food of the czars. Why eat like Stalin if you can eat like Peter the Great? He served us a thirteen-course tasting menu, from pumpkin soup to sea urchins, pausing at one point to chuckle and say, "I have borscht in my blood."

This, as we say in the business, is radio gold. By the end of two weeks in Russia we had a mountain of tape, much of it extraordinary. The trick when you're in the field is to draw a firm line for when it's time to hit pause on reporting and turn to filing. You have to force yourself to return to the hotel, lock yourself in your room, put room service on speed dial, and write. This is not my strong suit. There's always one more person you want to talk to, one more question you want to ask. You're out there in the world, witnessing fascinating events, speaking with fascinating people who are shaping their communities and their country. You want to keep talking with them, to record every story they can tell. But in order to share these stories with your listeners and readers—which is, after all, the point—you have to edit and fact-check and polish. You have to wrestle a forty-five-minute interview down to eight minutes, complete with translation and voiceovers, in order to fit the nonnegotiable timing requirements of *All Things Considered*.

The plan was to anchor the show live from Moscow on two nights, bookending the election and showcasing all our material. We had been filing bits and pieces along the way. But as deadline loomed, the bulk of that mountain of tape had yet to be conquered, and most of it was in Russian, so I wasn't much help. Sergei pitched in heroically, as did another interpreter we had hired for the trip, and also a couple of native Russian speakers back at headquarters. But the picture imprinted in my mind is of Monika, who had studied Russian all through school, and who is fiendishly gifted with languages, hunched over her laptop, sweating.

"Zashto da e lesno, kato moje da e trudno!" she cursed.

Moscow in March is eight hours ahead of Washington, which meant we were preparing to go live at midnight local time. As the evening wore on, and the vastness of the task still ahead became more clear, we recalculated over and over just how late we could push deadline without crashing the entire show. My editor and I were churning out copy, typing so fast smoke was surely flying from our fingers. Monika kept slogging. At one point, when a huge audio file froze on her laptop and then vanished, losing all her edits, she pushed back her headphones, looked up at me, and said, in a small voice, "I'm so stressed I'm vomiting inside my heart." Perhaps this also sounds better in Bulgarian.

I think of Mo and that trip sometimes when I'm struggling to talk with my boys. Why *should* things be easy when they can be difficult? Communicating with teenagers is so challenging. They're so unreasonable. I mention this to my mother one day, and her lips curve into a grin like a Cheshire cat.

"Oh, I wouldn't know. My children were angels when they were teenagers. Relentlessly communicative and pleasant."

She turns away and she's still grinning, for reasons I couldn't possibly fathom.

I think about how it isn't fair, when it's already so hard to talk with teenagers, that I can't hear mine half the time. I think about moments like the one with James at the kitchen sink. I'm sorry to say there have been many of those, and even sorrier to say they're far from the worst of it. We've had fights over small things, like whose turn it is to wheel the trash out to the curb. Also over big things, like the importance of telling the truth. We've had fights loud enough to shake the walls, fights that I fear neighbors at the end of the block had no trouble hearing. We both have a temper. He has always been deeply private, and fiercely independent, as am I. It's like trying to argue with a Mini-Me, except your Mini-Me has seven inches and fifty pounds on you.

What dawns on me, as I reflect on fighting about things that are not really the things we are fighting about, things like trash duty, or curfew, is . . . that recently the fight has gone right out of me. It no longer feels terribly important whether he makes curfew. Call the bad mothers brigade and report me, if you must. But since I began writing this book, this child has turned eighteen. This child, as he reminds me hourly, is now an adult. He can marry, he can vote, he can be called to fight and die for his country. Why am I wasting a single, precious second up on my high horse, insisting that so long as he lives under my roof, he lives by my rules, and that means getting home by one a.m.? Come to think of it, I might be close to abandoning my sixteen-year-old's curfew too. Alexander is more responsible than the rest of us combined; if anything, he's the one who should be laying down house rules.

Don't get me wrong: I want the boys to be accountable. I understand that teenagers need rules to push against. And of course it would be nice to have a soupçon of a clue as to their whereabouts as the clock strikes midnight on a Saturday night. But another, more important clock is also ticking. James is preparing to leave home, and Alexander is not far behind, and I am preparing to let them go. There will be no pushing this deadline. No faithful producer to intervene, edit the tape, and save the day.

This morning, I stood at the front door and waved, watching them reverse out of the driveway, all by themselves, to head to school and soccer practice. It was yesterday that they needed me as a chauffeur. Yesterday that I was strapping them into hulking corduroy car seats in the back seat, as they threw Goldfish crackers at each other and giggled and chattered.

Believe me when I tell you that it is a gift to be able to hear your children. A privilege to listen—really listen—to the people you love most in the world, giggling and chattering away. I regret moments that I wasted over the years, talking over them, scolding and correcting. *Is your homework done? Are you sure? What about your multiplication tables? Your summer reading? Your thank-you notes? Your college essays? Why haven't you packed? Why haven't you unpacked? Why aren't you in bed? Why aren't you up and dressed?*

Why . . . couldn't I pipe down and let them be?

Perhaps my work has conditioned me to be too quick to interrupt. Too quick to interrogate and fact-check and challenge. I think . . . I'm done. Ready to retire as disciplinarian and enforcer of house rules and schedules. What I find myself wanting to do in these last moments of their childhood is to go quiet and listen. To listen with no agenda, no judgment—only love.

The actual listening requires serious concentration. I have the best hearing aids money can buy, but for me, it is still hard work to hear. Carrying on a basic conversation can feel like trying to complete a word jumble, or a crossword puzzle, with the clues coming too fast. Nail down three down and seventeen across, and you realize you must have the answer to four down wrong. So you loop back to erase and fix it but meanwhile the clues keep coming, because the other person is still talking, and you're trying to keep up, scrambling to make sense of the mumbledy-mumbles flying past, desperate to fill in squares and lock down words so you can complete the section before they pause, tip their head, and inquire, "I mean, do you agree?" It's exhausting. Why should things be easy when they can be difficult?

The other part, though. The part about listening with no judgment, only love. Is it possible to love two boys exactly as they are, so fully that when their car rounds the corner and pulls out of sight, you feel your heart go with it?

Yes, indeed. And this, it turns out, is not difficult at all.

This, it turns out, is easy.

THE CALL

——◄•►——

It is 5:20 p.m. on a Friday afternoon, when my phone vibrates with an incoming call. This is unusual. My phone does not often ring between four and six p.m. on a weekday. Family and close friends know I'm likely to be on air, and they avoid the window.

I glance down and see that it is James calling. But I have to let it go to voicemail; I am at that moment reading a live intro to a piece about Trump's former chief of staff Mark Meadows, who was back in the headlines because he'd stopped cooperating with Congress's investigation into the January 6 insurrection and was now facing possible prosecution.

"NPR's Juana Summers reports . . . ," I finish reading, and then we hit the tape, which runs four minutes and thirty-three seconds. I return the call the moment my mic is clear.

"Hey, James. I'm on air. What's up?"

"Chicago 2026, baby!" he answers.

"Wait. No. NO. Really? You got in? Oh my God!"

And then we are both whooping for joy. The University of

Chicago is James's first choice. After we visited, James had announced his intention to apply early decision, which is binding—meaning if he gets in, he has to withdraw all other applications. Long gone are the days of waiting by the mailbox, hoping the envelopes arriving from colleges will be fat and not thin. James has received this news via his phone, while out with friends watching a high school basketball game. He is calling me from the bleachers, and I can hear a crowd of people around him stomping and cheering. For a moment it's easy to imagine they're celebrating for the same reason we are, that we're all in this together, that James's news is so wonderful and his excitement so infectious that the whole gym is joining us in a collective happy dance.

I hang up with James and attempt to refocus on the show that I'm still anchoring. Half an hour still to go. I have a live interview coming up, about a trial under way in Minneapolis for yet another white cop who has shot and killed yet another Black man during a traffic stop. There are ten minutes to prep, and I start skimming coverage of the trial, making sure I'm up to speed on what happened and what arguments both prosecutors and defense attorneys have laid out so far in court. The man was shot once in the chest with a 9-millimeter Glock. The officer who shot him—that she shot him is not in dispute—has testified that she yelled, "Taser! Taser! Taser!" but what she pulled was not her Taser but her gun.

I double-check a few more details in the draft script, including that we're pronouncing the dead man's name correctly. His name was Daunte Wright, pronounced *DAWN-tay*. But it's his age that stops me cold. Twenty. He was twenty. We have been covering his case since the beginning, but I had not until that moment taken in quite how young he was. Just two years older than James, neither of them old enough to buy a beer.

I think of his mother, of what it would be like to get that call. I look her up and read that she has testified already, that body cam video was presented in court, showing her arriving at the scene of the shooting, weeping, asking officers why her son had been shot. She testified that she could tell it was him, lying under a sheet beside his car, because she recognized his tennis shoes. I pull up Daunte's picture. He had a slim build and big eyes and he's wearing a red baseball cap with "Chicago" written across it.

I sit with this. Life is so staggeringly unfair. Why should one mother get a call delivering news of joy and another get a call delivering news of unimaginable horror? Why should one boy's life be cut short, when another boy's life and adventures are just beginning? The ways that we as a society and as a nation fail our children, particularly our children of color, are shameful.

I try to think what shoes James was wearing when he headed out the door this morning, whether I would recognize them. I think of his voice just now, so happy, relief and eagerness pulsing down the phone line. I send up a prayer for Daunte's mother, wherever she may be at that hour—*I am thinking of you; my heart hurts for you; I am so sorry.* Then I take a deep breath. Do the interview. Finish the show. Push back my chair, check my phone, think of my boys out in the world tonight, and pray that they will be safe.

LISTEN TO YOUR *OWN* MOM ON THE RADIO

——◆——

W HEN THE BOYS WERE SMALL, I WASN'T TIED TO ANY PARTICULAR SHOW ON NPR. My reports on intelligence and national security were as likely to air on *Morning Edition* as on *All Things Considered*. In the case of the former, unless the story was changing fast and there was a compelling reason to be awake and coherent at five or six a.m., I would try to complete my reporting, write it up, edit, and file it the night before. The next morning an anchor would read the intro to my piece live, and the engineer in the studio would hit the tape. This meant that in our home, where the radios are permanently tuned to NPR, the boys would often hear my voice holding forth on the news du jour, even as I was with them in the kitchen, pouring cereal and buttering toast.

One morning at preschool drop-off, another little boy greeted James by telling him he'd just listened to me on the drive to school. James stopped in his tracks, shot the boy a filthy look, and replied, "Listen to your *own* mom on the radio!"

All that day, I walked around wondering—Does he think all mothers are on air, running through the national headlines for their households during the morning breakfast hustle? It was a reasonable assumption, if you thought about it. Why should the routine at his friends' houses be any different from ours? Why not imagine an army of moms across America, delivering the daily news roundup before working in a plug to finish all the cantaloupe on the plate and then put the plate in the dishwasher? To this day, I have no idea when or how he figured out that other people—total strangers even!—could listen to me too.

The incident stands out because it was unusual for James to get territorial. Alexander was a more possessive child; for years he would nap only if snuggled firmly against Nick or me, his little arms wound tightly around our necks. James, on the other hand, was affectionate but preferred to do his own thing. I don't remember him crying when we left for work on weekday mornings, or when we dropped him at nursery school or at a birthday party. When the babysitter rang the doorbell on a Saturday night and the boys realized that Nick and I were going out, James was happy to see her. So long as pizza-and-movie night lay in his immediate future, he didn't particularly seem to care which benevolent adult was plunked on the couch beside him. (And he was wily enough to assess, correctly, that he had a better shot at wheedling ice cream out of her after the movie than he did with me.) Nick and I would start edging toward the door, and Alexander would be sulking and shooting daggers of betrayal from his eyes, and James would not throw us so much as a backward glance as he dragged the babysitter outside to show her his stick collection.

I was reminded of this—of his inherent non-clinginess—by a recent article by Ariel Levy in the *New Yorker*. The piece was about parenting, about a teacher who preaches a hands-off philosophy and trains adults to resist the modern urge to parent like a helicopter (constantly circling, constantly surveilling). I have mixed feelings about this. Nick and I lean more toward free-range parenting than a lot of our friends, but we're not immune to the impulse to hover. All I can tell you is, we love our kids, and we're doing our best.

The anecdote that prompted a moment of supreme recognition was about a two-year-old named Jasmine. She's gotten herself stuck on the second rung of a climbing structure at the playground, and now she's whining and calling for her parents to get her down.

They want to go to her, but the parenting guru suggests they give it a minute.

"Usually, if they can get there, they can get down from there," the guru counsels. Sure enough, moments later, Jasmine plucks up her courage and clambers down all by herself. Her relieved mother calls, "Jazzy, can I get a kiss?"

"Uh, nope," Jasmine calls back and wanders off.

I love this. It is exactly what James would have said at the age of two. It is exactly what he would say today, come to think of it. ("Have fun, Mom and Dad! Now, what's-your-name. Yeah, you. Want to see some sticks?")

IT IS BOTH A RELIEF AND A LITTLE DISCONCERTING TO REALIZE THAT YOUR KIDS ARE GOING TO TURN OUT THE WAY THEY TURN OUT, ALMOST NO MATTER WHAT YOU DO. We work so hard and love them so much and pour so much energy into parenting, but whatever impact we have really does seem to be at the margins. My boys have been raised in the same home, have attended the same schools, play the same sports, share the same gene pool. Yet they are so different, in looks and interests and personality. Clearly it's hardwired. As parents, we're just along for the ride.

This is helpful to remember, as the boys grow up and pull away. I would give a lot to cuddle tiny Alexander one more time, to feel his arms wound tight against my neck. I would give a lot to hang again with James and his stick collection, which to him were not sticks at all but a fearsome armory of—depending on the day—pirate swords, or Jedi lightsabers, or Robin Hood–style bows and arrows.

A perusal of our family photo albums from this era confirms that we all had our fantasies. There is one picture in particular that makes me laugh out loud. It's from the Halloween when they were two and four years old, so around the same time that James told his classmate to listen to his own mom on the radio. Both boys had decided to dress up as Spider-Man, in those padded costumes that fasten with Velcro up the back and bestow mighty shoulders and six-pack abs onto the frames of skinny toddlers. I, meanwhile, had gotten it into my head that year to make Dinner in a Pumpkin. I have a vague memory of getting the idea from some article, in one of those magazines targeting mothers that are always lurking like booby traps in the waiting rooms of pediatricians' offices and children's orthodontic practices. ("15 Fun Birthday Activities for a Sweet and Safe Celebration!" "Super Yummy Twists on PB&J That Your Kid Will Love!" "Make It an Unforgettable Halloween . . . with *Dinner in a Pumpkin!*")

It sounded delightful and easy and like the kind of thing the boys would remember all their lives, and always with gratitude that they were raised by such a wonderful, creative mother. So I made chili, following the suggested, exceedingly complicated recipe—a two-hour project in and of itself—then served it to the boys and their friends in cute little pumpkins that I had scooped out to use as bowls. The lids served as hats, and I used a Sharpie marker to draw age-appropriate, spooky yet not scary-looking jack-o'-lantern faces. I spent hours on those fucking pumpkins. The photo shows me, alone, smiling and demonstrating how to raise a pumpkin lid to reveal the tasty dinner inside. Not pictured: anyone actually eating Dinner from a Pumpkin, because no one did. The chili turned out weirdly sweet, no matter how much salt I threw in. Everyone, including me, swallowed a spoonful or two, pretended to like it, and then resumed mainlining Snickers Minis. The pumpkins went into the fridge "for another night." At some point, a week or so later, we threw them out.

I ask the boys. Neither has any memory of Dinner in a Pumpkin. (Thank God?) The lone surviving photo betrays none of the details I've just shared here. You could glance at it and conclude the pumpkins were not a flop but a huge hit, that what you're looking at marks the beginning of a favorite family tradition.

Photo albums document things exactly as they happened. But they do not show *everything* that happened. You get to throw out the pictures in which you have a double chin, or your eyes are shut, or your bra strap is showing. You get to pick the memories you keep. When the boys were small, I pressed photos into the crackling plastic sleeves of these faux leather albums that still line our bookshelves, and I didn't think much about how I was curating our family legend, the document that would survive to bear witness to what we were up to in 2007. What I created was both absolutely true . . . and a lovely fairy tale.

The pages show the boys dressed as Spider-Man, and then, as that fall and winter pressed on into spring, as Batman and Robin, as firefighters, as knights in armor. You see James and Alexander literally trying on and shedding identities, figuring out who they are, starting the process of growing into the young men they are now.

I am closing the album to replace it on the shelf when a question occurs to me, a question related to that weekend this past summer when I was in Georgia. It's still killing me a little that James hadn't missed me once, that I was away from home for a long weekend and he didn't even notice. I know it sounds petty, but it hurt. Much as I'm thrilled to have raised an independent, self-reliant kid, it made me pine for the good old days, the sweet, halcyon days of his childhood, when he never wanted to leave my side, when I was his whole world.

Ah, but . . . was I? I look hard at the pictures of four-year-old Spider-Man James. In one he's sticking his tongue out at the camera, and his eyes are dancing with mischief, and you can see his baby teeth are still intact. Would that boy have noticed if I disappeared for three days? Honestly, would he? So long as he was being well looked after, so long as his father and his brother and his babysitter—the nice one, the one who sneaked him ice cream—were around?

Could three days have passed before that kid looked up, puzzled, and asked, "Hey, hold on a minute, where's Mom?"

It brings a surprising amount of comfort to admit that I have no idea.

THIS WAS VLADIMIR PUTIN'S FAULT

———◄••►———

I AM RUMMAGING AROUND THE COAT CLOSET ON THE LANDING OUT-
SIDE JAMES'S ROOM, SEARCHING UNSUCCESSFULLY FOR MY FAVORITE
COAT. Then I remember. My coat is not there, because I lost it.
Two years ago, almost to the day, I left it draped across a chair at
the Tehran airport.

It was not a chic coat, mind you, not something you would
grab to look your best for a dressy night out. This was your basic
black trench coat, and it was almost certainly older than James. If
it had gone shapeless and shiny with age, it was also comfortable,
waterproof, and impossible to stain. Just the right length, not too
long and not too short. You couldn't wrinkle it if you tried, and
the armholes were cut to the perfect drop from my shoulders to
accommodate a backpack stuffed with documents and gear.

I had schlepped this coat all over the world on work trips.
When I finally abandoned it in the Tehran airport, at the gate
for a late-night Qatar Airways flight to Doha, it was not because
I meant to but because I was so desperately tired from a week
of round-the-clock reporting, surviving on two or three hours of

sleep, night after night after night, that I could barely remember my own name, much less my outerwear. I had collapsed into that chair and would have slept through boarding and last call for our flight had my producer not shaken me awake, dragged me upright, aimed me toward the plane, and pushed. Neither of us noticed the coat, still warm from my body, still on the chair.

Two years had passed since I'd missed it, because the pandemic had intervened. For two years we broadcast almost entirely from home. Forget roaming the world; I wasn't allowed even to set foot in my office in the newsroom, a few miles from my house, without advance permission and a very good reason. But now the latest Covid surge appeared to be ebbing, my team and I were vaccinated and boosted, and another conflict demanding coverage loomed. In the bleakest part of winter, January 2022, Russia had massed more than 100,000 troops on the border with Ukraine. Why? The Kremlin denied any plans to invade, but if what they said was true, what were all those troops and tanks doing there? Why were more continuing to arrive? Ukrainian citizen-soldiers began forming Territorial Defense Brigades, training in the streets. "We are prepared to defend our country," Ukraine's ambassador to the United States, Oksana Markarova, told me. "We will fight for our independence." The White House began warning of what could be the largest invasion since World War II.

Along with a handful of other NPR journalists, I had been pestering top editors about how we would cover the story. Very few global news organizations, NPR included, maintained full-time correspondents in Ukraine. Our International Desk started cycling people in, one at a time. Our Paris correspondent arrived, followed by our Berlin correspondent, both of them working closely with excellent Ukrainian "fixers," locals we hired to help with everything from translating, scheduling interviews, and fact-checking to booking train tickets, organizing drivers, and coaxing sleepy restaurant owners to stay open so we could grab a quick bite after meeting deadline.

As tensions escalated and diplomacy spluttered, I started pushing to bring a team and anchor the show live from the capital, Kyiv. We put in newsmaker interview requests, from Ukraine's president and foreign minister, to the chargé d'affaires who was running the American Embassy in Kyiv.

"If [the president] comes through and provides a centerpiece for our coverage, great," I wrote to my boss, the executive producer of *All Things Considered*. "But I'm wondering if things aren't getting so hot that we should be there anyway."

"Agree Ukraine feels pressing and worth pursuing," she replied the next day. She gave me the green light to assemble a team for travel, theoretically for two or three weeks down the road. But by the next day, the situation on the ground looked urgent. "Wondering if you'd consider going to Ukraine now," she wrote, and I understood that she meant *now*.

That was late on a Thursday. By Sunday, four of us were at the airport, holding boarding passes for Kyiv. Of the four, I was the only one with kids. My amazing producers did the heavy lifting on wrangling flight and hotel reservations, plus sourcing and packing the vast amount of recording, broadcast, and safety gear to pull off a trip like this. I focused on reading everything I could get my hands on, so I could ask good questions when we got there. And I focused on child care. I would be gone for at least nine or ten days. Nick had two work trips planned for the same window— domestic, so he wouldn't be far, but if you're not at home, you're not at home. And while the boys were teenagers and not toddlers, I was not comfortable leaving them for that long while I was overseas and headed to a potential war zone.

I called my mom and told her of my travel plans. She had two immediate questions. One was whether I had the right coat, so

I would be warm and look professional. Such a mom question. I told her I was mourning the loss of my trusty trench coat. I marveled that it had been two years since I'd gone anywhere, two years since I'd had occasion to need a coat for work. She made me promise to go shopping and find a worthy successor before my flight. Her other concern was for James and Alexander—"my boys," as she calls them.

"What about my boys?" she demanded. "Will Nick be there? You can't leave them for that long. I can come. I have an open schedule." This made my heart squeeze. It was true, and I knew the reasons. Dad was gone and no longer needed her to care for him around the clock. This was a relief, because caring for him was exhausting toward the end. But it was also terribly sad, both because she missed him and because it is hard to no longer be needed, when you have been a wife and best friend and caregiver for more than fifty years.

The other reason my mother's schedule was wide open was the pandemic. She was still being exceedingly careful, rarely leaving her house. She was scared to go to the grocery store, scared to attend her book club in person, scared to go to the gym or to get her nails done. But here she was volunteering, at the drop of a hat, to pack a bag, summon an Uber, trudge through the enormous Atlanta airport, and endure a crowded flight, to help me and to take care of her boys. I have an amazing mom. I have known this for a long time, have understood that I could not do half of what I do without her. I picked her up from the airport a few hours before my own flight took off. By the time I left again for my flight, she had set the table for dinner, ordered groceries for the week, and was busy teaching James to do his laundry without turning the whole load pink. She makes me want to be a better person.

James had a different set of questions when I told him I was headed to Ukraine.

"Is that safe?" he asked. "Where will you stay? What's the exit strategy? I just watched *Argo*. And what about the flight in? Can you just fly straight there?"

"Yes, it's easy," I assured him.

Famous last words.

I'M SWEATING AS I SETTLE INTO THE BACK SEAT OF MY UBER TO THE AIRPORT. My new coat is stiff and too hot, and I'm fighting the urge to tell my driver to turn around and take me home, so I can go back inside, hug my family, and build a pillow fort. Instead, I pull out my phone and check email.

Mistake.

Literally the first message, landed at the top of my inbox in the moments since I locked the front door behind me, has the following subject line: "REPORTABLE: State Department Orders Families of Kyiv Embassy Staff to Leave." ("Reportables" are notes from NPR editors to the entire news division, meant to communicate updates on fast-moving stories.) I click through the attached link to the State Department website. "**Do not travel to Ukraine due to the increased threats of Russian military action and COVID-19,**" it says in bold. A few sentences down it adds, "U.S. citizens in Ukraine should consider departing now using commercial or other privately available transportation options."

I opt not to forward this email to my mother or to James.

My itinerary is a ten-hour overnight flight to Istanbul, followed by a two-hour flight to Ukraine. Allowing for a layover and the time change, we will arrive at Kyiv's Borispol International Airport at dinnertime the following night. I sleep well on the first leg, and open my eyes to find the plane on its final descent, skimming

low over pristine, unpopulated mountains capped with snow.
Hmm. This is not how I remembered the approach to Istanbul, a
sprawling seaport of more than 15 million. It emerges that while
we've been in the air, a blizzard has walloped Istanbul. The airport has surrendered and shut down operations. Our plane has
been diverted to Dalaman, a resort town known for its mud baths
on Turkey's southern coast, a fact I learn only after we touch
down. Welcome to the perils of turning off your hearing aids so
you can zonk out on a long flight.

In the arrivals hall, we are told no flights will be going anywhere tonight. We queue for last-minute, cash-only Turkish visas
so we can leave the airport. We queue to retrieve our luggage, a
more protracted process than expected after the baggage carousel
jams and breaks down. I wonder privately if we are responsible.
On top of our personal suitcases and all our audio equipment,
we are muling oversized trunks stuffed with four spectacularly
heavy ballistic vests, four tactical helmets, four sets of protective
eyewear, and four first aid kits. You do not resent having to lug all
this gear around a conflict zone, where it can save your life. But
we are not in Ukraine, steeling for imminent invasion. We are in a
sleepy Turkish spa town in the off-season. We have not even managed to wrestle all the cases through customs before I am teaching
my producer and photographer that ever apt Bulgarian proverb:
Why should things be easy when they can be difficult?

That night we check into the tired but clean Dalaman Airport
Lykia Resort Thermal and Spa Hotel. The spa, alas, is closed. We
snag the last two rooms. I text my mom to let her know I'm safe,
before she sees my Twitter feed and worries. "Sleep tight," she
replies. "Glad you got a new warm coat."

From there, a comedy of complications proceeds to unfurl.

We've been asking when the rescheduled flight to Istanbul

might depart, and while we're at dinner, someone slides a note under the doors to our rooms. "Dear Guest," it reads. "TK 8 America passengers. Pick up time 08:00."

That seems fine. During the night, though, a second note silently appears under the door: "Dear Guest. TK 8 America passengers. Pick up time 08:00 canceled."

That's it. No other information, no word on a new time.

We hedge our bets and buy an alternate flight, this one connecting through the capital, Ankara, in case Istanbul takes a while to dig out. We're back at the Dalaman airport before dawn, patting ourselves on the back for this genius move. We've just managed to drag our bags through the first security screening and over to the check-in desk when . . . the Departures board updates. Our Ankara flight is canceled. We survey our options: a total of eight flights are scheduled to depart this airport today. I'm willing to take any of them, just to make some progress. We buy coffee and pastries and set up camp. Oh, the innocence. All morning my colleagues and I take turns shuttling between the Turkish Airlines check-in desk, where they have no information, and the Turkish Airlines ticket counter, where a kind man who is optimistic to the point of delusional tells us to stay put, that new flights could be announced at any moment.

My producers start canceling interviews in Kyiv that we are clearly not going to make. We postpone the former prime minister of Ukraine, and a member of parliament. I call NPR's Istanbul correspondent, Peter Kenyon, and beg for help, though even I'm not clear on what exactly he's supposed to do to fix this situation. I tell him we want to rent a car and drive to Istanbul; we could make it in nine or ten hours. He reads me dispatches from Turkish newspapers detailing how thousands of people across the country are stranded in cars and buses, because main roads are also paralyzed by snow. This persuades me not to rent a car, but moves us no closer to a plan to get out of here. Around lunchtime, even the optimistic ticket-counter man gives up. The lights in the terminal switch off. The coffee shop closes. We are told to return to the hotel and await further instruction.

"Ukraine, we are trying to get to you!" I tweet from back at the good old Lykia Resort Thermal and Spa Hotel. We are handed the keys to our old rooms. "Flights Have Been Canceled Until Tomorrow," reads a sign posted in the lobby. "You Can Continue to Stay at the Hotel."

Hope dims. More snow is forecast for tonight; who's to say anything will in fact improve tomorrow? But then Kenyon calls. He has been working his contacts and he produces a name, Elif, and a cell phone number. Elif is a Turkish travel agent who may have been a saint in a past life. She listens to our tale of woe. Within the hour she has found us a local driver and a van, which will shuttle us and our hundreds of pounds of gear for the three-and-a-half-hour drive along icy, twisting mountain roads to Antalya, the location of another regional airport on the Mediterranean coast, which is allegedly open, and which allegedly has a 9:30 p.m. flight to the airport in Ankara, which allegedly has a midnight connection to Kyiv. This all sounds like a verrrry long shot. But what else are we doing this afternoon?

"Trying to get to Ukraine, plan #17," I tweet from the very pretty drive across southern Turkey. Snow is everywhere. Families are sledding and throwing snowballs. For a moment it feels so good to be out in the world again, after two years of pandemic lockdown, that I scarcely care whether we make it onto a plane tonight or not.

But our driver prevails over the icy roads. At Antalya airport, the lights are on. Our flight is on time. We board; we take off; we land. One down. "Oh hello Ankara airport," I tweet. "A fine airport in a city I look forward to visiting again someday. But for now . . . changing gates to catch a midnight flight to Ukraine. #NeverGiveUp."

I think of James and Alexander. Of the life lessons we try to pass on to our children. Also of the weekend, years ago now, that our family spent in Istanbul. How the boys had marveled at the food and sights, the skyline of minarets and skyscrapers. Alexander had fallen in love with orange blossom–flavored Turkish delight and with the stray dogs that roam the city. James had perked up inside Topkapi Palace, where he wanted details—*all* the details—on how the Ottoman sultans and their harems had functioned.

I wonder what would catch their eyes today. I wonder if we should book another trip here, maybe a family vacation week this summer. Will James even agree to come on a family vacation, or will he want to do his own thing, the summer after his senior year? Maybe if we offer to bring his girlfriend with us? Questions for another day. For now, I buckle my seat belt, close my eyes, and brace to take off, finally, for Ukraine.

✳

THERE ARE MANY WAYS TO TELL THE STORY OF A WAR. But one of the best is to go there, find the ordinary people whose lives have been upended, and listen.

It has taken me time to learn this, because I love the high-level, wonky policy stuff. I am in my element grilling, say, the secretary general of NATO on the principle of collective defense. But like any lofty principle, the reason it matters, ultimately, is how it affects individual people and their lives. Nations commit themselves to a pact that an attack against one is an attack against all so that within each of their borders, within every town, on street after street, in house after house, families can sleep safe and secure at night. That's the point. That's what all the highfalutin stuff boils down to, whether you're talking collective defense or a nuclear nonproliferation treaty or climate change or multilateral counterterrorism cooperation. I try to remember this, every time I roll into a new city to cover a story, even—or perhaps especially—the big ones, the stories with massive diplomatic and military stakes. In Kyiv every morning, I would wake up, plug in my coffee pot, and then, while my coffee brewed, gaze out my hotel window at all the apartments out there, all the kitchen lights flicking on as dawn broke, all the people inside, waking up to make their own coffee and walk their dogs and brush their teeth and run their kids to school. Ordinary people trying to live their lives as best they could, as are we all.

Our second morning in Ukraine, we headed to parliament to interview Ivanna Klympush-Tsintsadze. She was feisty and outspoken even by politician standards, so much so that it was hard at first to get a word in edgeways. She chaired the parliamentary Committee on Ukraine's Integration into the European Union. An EU flag sat on the round conference table in her office, and she sipped her coffee from a NATO mug. We talked sanctions, and whether Germany should be shipping more arms to Ukraine. We talked about domestic political fault lines; she was not a fan of Ukraine's president, Volodymyr Zelenskyy. But the moment I locked on was when I asked her about being a mom, and I discovered that she also had two teenagers. How was she talking to them about everything that was going on?

Ah, she sighed. "Tough conversations."

She had been trying to explain to her younger daughter, age fifteen, that if war came, they might have to separate. Her daughter would be sent to stay with grandparents, while the "grown-ups will have to take weapons and try to defend the country."

"She was asking me, 'Mom, could you promise me that, first

and foremost, you are not a politician, but first and foremost, you are my mom—and you will—if something is happening, you will, first and foremost, take care of me?'" Klympush-Tsintsadze brushed away a tear. "That was the toughest conversation I've had up till this particular moment because I had to explain that, listen, I have responsibility."

I wanted to make sure that I understood her correctly. "You're looking at whether you need a gun to defend yourself, your home?"

"The country," she said, nodding. "That will be the . . . last resort for us to defend the country."

I imagined what it would be like to have such a conversation with Alexander, how furious and frightened he would be. It drove home to me the stakes of this showdown at the Ukraine-Russia border more forcefully than the discussion of sanctions ever could have. Listening from my home in Washington, my mother had a similar reaction. She had cooked shrimp pasta for Nick and the boys that night, and had been subjected to their usual torrent of soccer news. "Dinner talk focused on a lot more sports than I'm used to," she texted. Then she brought up the interview with Klympush-Tsintsadze; she had listened after she went up to bed.

"Interesting discussion about her children and feeling she might need to have a gun to defend her country and her family," Mom wrote. "The personal thoughts bring it home."

The next day I took an Uber to a popular pizzeria, to meet another formidable woman. Hanna Hopko had also served in Ukraine's parliament. She chaired the powerful foreign affairs committee, having made a name for herself as one of the original leaders of the Euromaidan protests that toppled the government in 2014. We drank tea and ate veggie pizza, and I listened as she spoke with passion about the national spirit that fed the revolution, how she had felt part of something larger than herself.

Hopko was so impressive and so determined that I began to

wonder why she had served only five years in parliament, why she had decided not to run for reelection and had instead shifted recently to what seemed a lower-profile job. Had she lost her idealism and conviction that change was possible? Could she no longer see a way to help her country from inside the government? No, no. Hopko brushed my question aside. Nothing like that. It was because she was working so hard that she never saw her daughter.

Speaking of whom, she told me, this daughter was now eleven years old and begging for a guinea pig. She had earned it, Hopko conceded. Her daughter had excellent grades. But if bombs started falling on Kyiv, they would need to evacuate. The thought of having to pack and run with a rodent, along with its cage and all its food, was seriously stressing Hopko out. Still, she was weakening. This was Vladimir Putin's fault, this mess. Hopko banged her fist on the table. "Putin's fault! Not my daughter's fault! Why should she be punished?"

KELLY: Oh, my goodness.

HOPKO: We will manage to buy.

KELLY: (Laughter) I don't mean to laugh, but I am picturing you having to evacuate with a guinea pig.

HOPKO: (Laughter) So this is like a family story.

KELLY: Wow—so one more thing to worry about . . .

HOPKO: Yeah.

KELLY: . . . If it all goes terribly wrong. Oh, dear. Oh, and you're crying.

It was true. I was crying too. Hanna Hopko, fierce leader of a national revolution who went on to serve her country in parliament, was weeping at the thought of having to evacuate her home, with her daughter and a guinea pig in tow. I sat there, trying to hold it together, and thought how there was not a mother on this planet who would not relate.

"Beautiful big snowflakes coming down," my own mother texted that night from Washington. Then: "I loved the guinea pig Mom. We all love our children."

"Yes," I replied. Yes. We sure do.

THE SECOND HALF OF OUR TIME IN UKRAINE, WE TRAVELED EAST. Six hours by train from Kyiv, and then another three or four by car. This is another thing I've learned about covering conflict: if at all possible, get out of the capital. You will glimpse a very different picture of what's happening and why, once you venture outside the big city.

In Ukraine's eastern Donbas region, people looked at you funny if you asked whether they were worried about war with Russia. This is because they were already living it. Russian-backed separatists had moved in and declared breakaway republics in 2014. Ukrainian forces fought back. The war had been stalemated for years. The front lines rarely moved. But the two sides had carried on shelling and shooting at each other ever since.

We met one old man who lived just a few miles from the Russian border, who asked us to identify him only by his middle name, Davydovych, because he was worried he would be recognized, worried about repercussions. He spoke Russian, the first language of most people in this part of Ukraine. He pointed at bombed-out houses up and down his block; nearly all his neighbors had fled or been killed.

"On that street, the man died there. The woman died there," he told us, his eyes shifting from one front door to the next. We'd been warned to stay on hard pavement in his neighborhood, not to step onto grass; there were still active land mines. What would he do if more fighting came? I asked.

"I don't know," he said. "I'm just fed up with it. I'm broken inside."

Davydovych had heard gunfire nearby just that morning. He wasn't sure from which direction, or who was doing the shooting. He sighed in a way that suggested he'd given up trying to keep track. When we made to leave, he walked with us, still talking, words tumbling out, like a man who had forgotten what it was like to have people around to listen.

To get this close to the front required passing through a series of military and police checkpoints. Guards wielding Kalashnikovs checked our press IDs and passports at each roadblock. We had no problems. We heard no shooting. But military vehicles passed us on the roads, and we could see trenches dug into the frozen fields around us, like a tableau from 1914. We each carried in one of those heavy ballistic vests, along with helmets and shatterproof eye protection and field first aid kits.

I had put off telling my mother about this stage of the trip. I knew she would be concerned. She had enough to manage, trying to hold down the fort with the boys and the Bernedoodle in Washington. But if someone volunteers to take care of your home and your family, they deserve to know where you are. And so, on the way in, from the train rolling through flat, snowy grain fields, I had emailed. "Letting you know we are on a train to eastern Ukraine," I wrote. I told her about the colleagues I was traveling with, how smart and experienced they were, what stories we hoped to report, and when we would return to Kyiv.

"Not sure what cell service will be like," I added, "so don't worry if I don't reply right away."

I knew how this would go down. She would become a one-woman news service of articles on Donbas, forwarding snippets and travel advisories, enough to give our newsroom reference librarians a run for their money. She would be quietly terrified for my safety and that of my team. But she would say nothing to the boys, and she would say nothing to me beyond wishing me luck on my assignment.

It was the middle of the night in Washington, but her reply to my note came back in just nine minutes: "Thank you for letting us know. My love and prayers." Fourteen minutes later, she followed up with the first of several articles about the status of Russian troops at the border. I was skimming through them, when one of my producers sent a text. A logistics update, alerting my colleagues and me to the latest on the ground support team that would meet us. Between the first and second checkpoints, our first driver would swap with a new one, who would take us the rest of the way to the front line. She notes the new driver's mobile number and his name, Oleksander. I think immediately of my own Alexander. My beautiful red-haired boy, Alexander Nicholas, who carries the names of not one but two Russian czars. I have also been texting him from the train, reminding him of Shadow's grooming appointment that afternoon at the doggie day spa in DC. There is no multitasker like a mother in a war zone.

I sit back, stare out the window at the rusty Soviet-era train cars flying past on a parallel track, and think about next chapters. I am older than my colleagues on this trip, by an average of two decades. My physical stamina is fine. Running helps. And I'm full of ideas. But they have to coax me to try new software; one of my producers patiently installs the latest update of the Google Drive app on my phone and ignores my complaints as she teaches me how to use it. Then there's my mini-Marantz audio recorder, the one I have carried all over the world and have been using here in Ukraine. It is the tech equivalent of my beloved trench coat. It has never failed me. You will have to pry it, hopefully many years from now, from my cold, dead hands. But it is apparently so antique that none of my twenty- or thirty-something colleagues can figure out how to upload the contents of the sound card to their laptops, and I have helpfully left the relevant cable back at the hotel in Kyiv. Have I become that person? The codger who clings to ancient technology because they're superstitious and wary of upgrading to newer, faster models? Why, yes, apparently, I have.

Meanwhile, my kids. In two years and change, both my sons will be out of the house. There will be no need to fly my mother up to Washington to keep watch. No need to plan carpools or meals in my absence. I'll be free to travel, with no guilt about leaving my children, for the first time in twenty years.

Will I still want to? Am I getting too old for this? How will I know?

WE ARE DRIVING WEST, PASSING BACK THROUGH THE SAME CHECKPOINTS WE CLEARED ON THE WAY INTO DONBAS, MAKING OUR WAY TO THE SLOVYANSK STATION TO CATCH AN OVERNIGHT TRAIN TO KYIV, WHEN HANNA HOPKO TEXTS.

"Thank you and your team for lovely interview," she writes. "I received many exciting feedbacks." She attaches a batch of photos. They begin in a pet store and end in what appears to be her apartment, and they feature a plump white-and-brown guinea pig in a large brand-new plastic crate.

"It's so cute," Hopko writes. Some of the photos show her daughter, who is also pretty cute: round glasses, long hair escaping from beneath a fuzzy gray hat. She is setting up the crate and grinning from ear to ear.

I look at these pictures and see two things. The first is hope. No matter how devoted a parent you are, you don't buy your eleven-year-old a guinea pig, complete with crate and bedding and water bottle and bags of food pellets, if you really believe Vladimir Putin and his troops are about to lay siege to your city. This hypothesis is confirmed when Hopko writes again, saying that while the family is of course preparing for a range of scenarios, "we truly believe the guinea pig will stay in Kyiv."

The second thing I see in these photos is love. War or no war, I don't believe that Hanna Hopko needed a guinea pig in her life any more than allergic, dog-averse me needed a puppy named Shadow in mine. But when a person you love beyond all reason is begging, your own needs and desires can begin to feel irrelevant. Children demand things that make life so much more complicated and expensive. But they also fill life with love and wonder; they do crazy, exasperating, glorious things that will become the stories we will tell their children and their children's children, when we are old enough to be great-grandparents.

There is no question that I interview people differently because I am a mother. Being a mother has changed which stories feel worth telling. My twenty-something self might have showed up to interview Hopko armed with the latest, coolest high-tech recorder, but she would never have pressed on the guinea pig line of questioning. She would have switched gears and redirected the conversation to the "important" stuff, to the latest diplomatic and military machinations. Who cares whether some random kid gets a pet, when a continent's armies are on the move? But the guinea pig . . . it IS the story. It's what you will remember from that interview with the fearless Hanna Hopko, the next time you turn on your radio and there's an unsettling development in Ukraine.

"But are the little girl and her guinea pig okay?" you'll ask.

And hopefully I'll have an answer for you.

✳

RIGHT BEFORE WE BOARD THE SLEEPER TRAIN WEST, BACK TOWARD KYIV AND THE INTERVIEWS THAT AWAIT US THERE THE NEXT MORNING, A TEXT ARRIVES FROM MOM. I know that she is writing because she is worried. She wants to make sure that I am safe, that I haven't lost my coat again, that I'm on my way back to the relative safety of the capital.

She writes none of this.

"I made a huge pot of spaghetti sauce," she reports. "There is some in the freezer for the boys on another day. It's very cold here; the snow hasn't melted. Shadow and Nick are watching TV together. We miss you but we're doing okay."

I read between the lines. I have been corresponding with my mother for a lifetime, and in what might seem a simple status update, I detect several subtexts.

Yes, this is a gentle nudge to check in.

It is also a quiet assertion of competence. She would like for me to know that she is doing splendidly, that she is running my house with a grace and efficiency from which both I and the military commanders on the front lines that I have just left behind might learn much.

But what I also read—and maybe I'm just seeing what I need to see—is encouragement, and permission. *You have chosen such a different life than I did*, she is writing. *Go live it. Go do your thing. James and Alexander are fine; they are happy; their bellies are full of spaghetti. I've got this. You are free to go get 'em.*

A mother's love is such a powerful force. It can wire courage across thousands of miles, straight into a war zone. If you are very lucky, it can score you a Bernedoodle, or a guinea pig.

That night I lie on my narrow berth, in the tiny compartment I am sharing with my producer, swaying as the train wheels rumble underneath. Strange towns whip past in the dark. I close my eyes and try to sleep. I am thinking of all the people we have met on this trip, of how they have trusted us with their stories, of how to write my report tomorrow in a way that is true and fair and does them justice.

And I am thinking of my mother, and how we pay it forward.

THE FORCES OF NATURE

———•◦•———

THERE IS A SUPPORTING CAST TO THIS STORY TO WHOM YOU HAVE NOT YET BEEN INTRODUCED: MY FEMALE FRIENDS. They have helped me raise these boys.

You reach the age of fifty, and if you're lucky, you have forged and sustained friendships from many stages of life. In my case: from childhood, from high school, from new mommy playgroups. Also from soul-killing overnight shifts in the newsroom, and from mornings shivering together on the kids' soccer sidelines. From book club, and from around the neighborhood, and from sweating and giggling on adjacent mats in yoga class.

But for our purposes here, I want to focus on my college roommates.

There are eleven of us. Christina, Jess, Kat, Kate, Kathy, Kerry, Meg, Paula, Sasha, Tracy, and me. Privately, and a little sheepishly, we refer to each other as the FONs—the Forces of Nature. Our husbands came up with this moniker, so many years ago that they may have enjoyed mere boyfriend status at the time, and I choose to believe it was meant affectionately. They were trying to capture that we were unpredictable and a lot of trouble but definitely not boring.

Quite how this group came together and became so tight-knit, I can't recall. Also, fact check: while we tell people we were roommates, because it's the most succinct way of capturing the closeness of our relationship, and while we did all graduate from college together in 1993, we did not all technically live together. Meg was assigned to a different dorm than the rest of us. Jess started out in a different class year. She's the only one with whom I ever actually shared a shower and a soap dish, and that was only for senior year. Nor do we all live near each other today. There are clusters around Boston and New York. I'm the only one to have settled in Washington, DC. One of us lives in Maine, another in San Diego, literally opposite corners of the country, as far north-east and as far southwest as you can get in the continental United States.

I think our bond has something to do with the precise moment at which we launched our adult lives and careers. Had we graduated five years earlier, none of us would have had an email account or a cell phone. Long-distance calls would have been prohibitively expensive. But all that was changing in the boom years of the mid-1990s, and suddenly it was easy to keep chattering away just as we always had. This week alone, our group text thread has lit up with Kat sharing a *Guardian* article she feels we need to read, with Paula sharing details of the funeral arrangements for her sweet father, with Kate reminding us to wish Kathy a happy birthday, with Jess reminding Kate that Kathy's birthday isn't in fact until the next day, and with Kathy ignoring both of them and sharing a math joke that has her kids cracking up. The thread rarely goes quiet for more than a day or two.

The other thing that keeps us close is that we gather, in person, at least once a year. For a long time, these fly-ins were centered on weddings. Then baby showers. Recently, it's been fiftieth birthday parties. There is a two-year age gap between the oldest and the youngest FON, and Paula was the first to hit the midcentury mark. She pulled off what none of us knew would be the last dinner party for a long time: a beautiful, intimate feast of three courses, lit up by candlelight and too much wine and the banter of very old friends telling very old, very inside jokes. Along with our partners, we were squeezed into the garret of a tiny French restaurant in New York, a space that would comfortably have held half our number. We sat pressed elbow to elbow, so close we mixed up our wine glasses and sampled food off each other's plates, swapping forks back and forth and licking each other's spoons, just as we had in the dining hall three decades before. It was February 29, 2020. The coronavirus was spreading like wildfire in New York, though we didn't grasp that yet. Social distancing and masks were still in our future; not even the doctor among us was wearing one yet. That night, in hindsight, feels like the gilded, shimmering end of the Before Times, before the curtain dropped and everything was overtaken by plague.

Miraculously, no one got sick at Paula's party. Months passed. One by one, more of us turned fifty. We made each other birthday videos and convened over Zoom. It was not the same. Every time it seemed we might be turning a corner and leaving the pandemic behind, a new variant hit. Almost all of us were caring for children or for elderly parents or both, and it didn't feel safe to gather in real life.

Finally, two years to the month after Paula's soirée, with everyone vaccinated and boosted, we decided it was time. Sasha and Kat, the youngest of the FONs, were finally turning fifty. They hatched a plan to descend on Scottsdale, Arizona, for a long weekend, no husbands invited this time. I believe the rationale was that Scottsdale would be reliably sunny and warm, that we could rent a house with a hot tub out the back door for less than what a single hotel room in New York would cost, and that it was inconvenient . . . for everyone. Equal opportunity complaining about delayed flights, lost luggage, and the general ickiness of traveling in the Omicron era.

We hiked long rocky trails through the desert. We got our culture in, an art-and-architecture tour of Frank Lloyd Wright's stunning compound Taliesin West. We compared frown lines and bunions. We talked about books we were reading, and about politics, and about sex and careers and weeknight chicken recipes. We interrupted each other constantly, completing each other's thoughts and changing the subject, so that hardly any story ever reached an end. Someone insisted on playing a parlor game called Celebrity. I never figured out the rules, partly because we kept arguing over and changing them, but toward the end it deteriorated into something recognizable as charades, with Kate doing what appeared to be a very authentic impersonation of a chicken.

"Guys!" she finally erupted, after we failed to guess for a full five minutes. "*Come on.* How are you not getting this? It's Mitch McConnell."

I laughed until I couldn't breathe, falling against Meg on the sofa beside me, my chest aching, still laughing, and still I couldn't breathe, until I began to wonder whether I might be having a mild heart attack.

Paula had brought everyone copies of a self-help book. The title was *Goddesses Never Age*, and it promised that the best was yet to come. There were chapters on eating ("Goddesses Savor the Pleasure of Food"), exercise ("Goddesses Move Joyously"), and owning our beauty (Goddesses Are Gorgeous"). Some of the tips were hokey; some constituted excellent advice.

The book concluded with something called "The 14-Day Ageless Goddess Program." Day One kicked off with, "Don't Act

Your Age!" By Day Six, we had moved on to instructions for creating a sensual playlist and reconnecting with our pelvic bowls, which was not as intriguing as it sounds ("Swing your hips or belly dance to music").

I looked around me, at these women whose faces and voices were as familiar to me as my own. The maid of honor at my wedding was here, as was the godmother of my oldest child. These women had been cheering me on and picking me up when I fell for more than half my life. These women would drop everything and get on a plane to help me if I needed them; I knew this because they had done it. None of us looked twenty anymore. But how were we possibly old enough to be reading self-help books for mature women?

I closed the book. Nope. Not there yet. I wandered into the kitchen and asked Jess to make me a mojito. She made it strong. She started telling me a story that had me laughing again. I looked at her. She was beautiful. I decided we were already divine goddesses. We were doing fine. If there was any group of people on earth I would be happy to stand with as a mature woman, this was it. But at the rate Jess had me cackling and knocking back rum, "maturity" might not be the first word you would associate with us.

I resolved to take the book home, stick it high on a shelf somewhere, and pull it down again in a decade, on the occasion of our sixtieth birthdays. Maybe we would be ready for it then. Maybe.

✳

RECENTLY I INTERVIEWED ANN PATCHETT, OF *BEL CANTO* AND *STATE OF WONDER* FAME. I told her that she was my favorite author, that I would read anything she ever wrote, to which she replied that she was verklempt. If you, like me, just had to furtively google that, it means "overcome with emotion." The finest writers among us are constantly enriching our vocabulary, even when we're not reading their books but merely chitchatting with them down a phone line.

The occasion for our interview was the publication of her latest collection of essays, *These Precious Days*. Patchett is as perceptive and prolific in penning her memoirs as she is with writing her novels. (This is another thing about the finest writers among us: many of them are annoyingly good at both fiction and nonfiction.) We talked about trying to write during a pandemic, and about how we both had lost our fathers after long illnesses, how we felt sorrow but also blessed release, the two emotions intertwined. And we talked about friendship. The title essay was about a remarkable woman whom Patchett had gotten to know only recently, when they were both in middle age.

KELLY: You write that what you loved was finding someone who sees you as your best and most complete self. And that she did that for you, and you think you did that for her. And it's so unexpected, to come across a friendship like that at this point in life.

PATCHETT: It really is. And certainly, I have made some close friendships as an adult. But there is a quality of youthful friendship that is based on wasting time together, having just whole days where you're not making plans.

This rings so true. In my experience, the bond with college roommates is forged less when you're engaged in anything constructive than over the many nights when you're up together in the wee hours raiding the fridge, procrastinating on a paper due at nine a.m. that you've had three weeks to write, and arguing over whether it would be a good idea to get the name of the cute guy you snogged last weekend tattooed on your left ankle (answer, for any current college students out there reading this: No. Very bad idea). I watch James and Alexander and their high school buddies, watch them cementing lifelong friendships rooted in the delightful pursuit of wasting time together.

My sons are already in that phase of life when their friends are everything. For me, it began around seventh or eighth grade and lasted, if we're being completely honest here, through my twenties. It wasn't that I didn't like my parents during these years, just that I didn't spend much time thinking about them or asking if they wanted to hang out on Saturday night. But a funny thing happened not long after I hit thirty. My career was intense and demanding. I had a baby, then another. And as wonderful and supportive as my friends were and remain, their lives were increasingly frenetic too. Not one of them was volunteering to come keep the boys for a long weekend so that Nick and I could get away. Not one of them begged us to come live with them, that hard winter when Alexander was a newborn and James was a toddler and for three months, while our house was being renovated, we didn't have a place to live. Nope, that was Mom and Dad.

In my thirties and into my forties, I still texted and talked to the FONs all the time. But it was my mom I wanted on the other end of the phone line when one of the boys spiked a fever and I was scared. It was my dad who would sling them over his shoulder and walk, for hours. That winter that we lived with my parents in Georgia, Alexander was colicky and never slept. Dad would report for duty in bathrobe and slippers, his only questions where the diapers were and if there was a bottle ready to go in the fridge. The two of them would prowl around the darkened house, Dad whispering stories of Reddy Fox and Spot the loyal sheepdog, the same stories he had told my brother and me when we were very small, until Alexander's howls quieted and they both grew sleepy. I would find them passed out together, peacefully snoring, in Dad's favorite armchair.

The older you get, the more you realize time is not a line but a circle. Everything comes around again. My parents were the center of my world until they weren't, until my teens and twenties, when my friends were everything. Then came babies and needing my parents again with an urgency I had not felt since I was a child myself. And meanwhile Mom and Dad were getting older, and then Dad got sick, and they began to need me in ways they had not foreseen either. Family reasserted itself at the center of my world.

These last eighteen years since James and then Alexander were born, my role as a mother has defined me. Being their mother has been and will always be the most important work of my life. But as the years pass, it consumes fewer of my waking hours. It's already been years since they needed Nick and me to bathe them or dress them or read to them. They pour their own cereal in the mornings. They put themselves to bed at night. And the weekends. Our weekends have been dominated by the boys' needs and activities, mostly soccer, for so long that I really can't imagine facing a Saturday and thinking, *What shall I do today? How shall I pass the time?*

Soon, though, it will be just Nick and me and Shadow on the weekends. So many free hours loom. Time for long walks with girlfriends, and Bloody Mary brunches, and meeting a friend at a museum, and more getaways like the weekend at Scottsdale. This sounds—dare I say it?—kind of great.

ONE OF THE FONS WITH WHOM I AM CLOSEST, KAT, HAS A SON WHO WAS BORN TWO MONTHS AFTER JAMES. His name is Will. They are friends. They've grown up in different cities, but we sent them away together to summer sleepaway camp, where they bunked in the same cabin and thus became the second generation of roommates between our two families. Her younger son, Grant, is buddies with Alexander. They have also bunked together, same summer camp.

The boys delight in teasing Kat and me, among other things, for our allegedly ruthless campaigns to starve them over the entire duration of their childhood by purchasing only aggressively healthy and nutritious food. The last time we were at Kat's house for dinner—cheeseburgers on the grill and ice cream for dessert, for the record—Will dragged James into the kitchen to lament the cereal selection.

"Look," he said, peering into the cupboard. "Organic muesli. Puffed kamut. What even is that? What is kamut?"

"Is it even food?" James asked, in solidarity.

"For gerbils, maybe."

"You should see what my mom buys. Lots of bran. No sugar. The worst."

In my defense, I'll note that my anti–Frosted Flakes stance did not survive the pandemic. Even I was eating them. All the rules went out the window. To this day, surplus bags of Tater Tots from Trader Joe's line our freezer; I bought so many that the boys grew weary of them. (They are delicious, especially doused with extra salt and dipped in barbecue sauce. Don't tell Kat.)

Will came to stay with us for a few nights this past summer, when he was visiting colleges nearby. James and Alexander were both out of town on various summer projects, so we put him up in Alexander's bedroom, which was as usual considerably tidier than his big brother's. Will arrived by car. Correction: he attempted to arrive by car. He had driven from Boston to Washington by himself, in the family's beloved clunker, a 2006 Toyota High-lander hybrid named Steve with 150,000 miles on it. Steve made it without incident all the way from New England only to overheat and break down on Dupont Circle, a few blocks from our house. We helped Will get Steve towed to the garage at the end of our street.

The quote for repairs came in the next day and was predictably eye-popping. New parts were required, and they were going to take a few days to arrive, so we lent Will the keys to James's car, which was gathering dust and blocking my car in the driveway anyway. The college road trip continued. Will returned the car at the end of the week with a full tank of gas, cleaner than he'd found it, and he even located James's long-missing driver's license when he vacuumed under the passenger seat.

There is something so wonderfully full circle about this. About Kat's son driving my son's car to visit colleges, one of which he might attend, and where he might meet the roommates who, if he is very lucky, will become HIS lifelong friends.

I met Kat when I was eighteen, the age that James and Will are now. We were close in college and have grown closer in the three decades since we graduated. Read my will and you will find a section stating that if anything were ever to happen to both Nick and me, and should our parents be unable to step in, Kat and her husband would take our children and raise them. It's the hugest, most personal thing you can imagine asking of someone. And it occurs to me that this is yet another thing ending, another arrangement about to be outgrown. At eighteen, James is now too old to require a guardian should something befall his parents. He is now legally free to live wherever and with whomever he likes. Alexander is right behind him. It's exactly how things should be and it is also totally terrifying.

After James heard from the University of Chicago, I texted Kat. I knew she would want to know, no matter what was happening with Will's applications, even if he had not gotten good news.

Had they heard anything yet? I asked. We were rooting for Will, I told her. Whatever happened, things would all work out, and both boys would end up somewhere great. She wrote back immediately with a string of happy emojis. Will had just been accepted at his first choice too—amusingly, not one of the ones he'd driven Steve the clunker down to see, but a university that's all of a fifteen-minute walk from their house.

I thought about the two boys, headed off to freshman year. How it felt like a lifetime ago but also like yesterday that Kat and I had moved into our freshman dorms and found each other.

"How do we have CHILDREN old enough to go to college?" I ask. "How did this happen???"

"It's totally insane and bonkers," she writes back. "We're not old enough for this to be the case!!"

She's right. We're not. But, somehow, here we are.

RETIREMENT

————————

I'M NOT GOING TO PLAY," JAMES ANNOUNCES.

We are eating dinner, panfried chicken and mashed pota-
toes, the four of us in our usual seats around the kitchen table.
James is wearing tartan flannel pajama bottoms and a maroon
UChicago T-shirt, which is to say, his new uniform. He has not
been spotted sans college logo gear since shortly after the acceptance letter for the class of 2026 arrived.

When we had visited the campus, James and I walked over to
the stadium to watch a varsity soccer game. I heard him catch his
breath as he settled onto the bleacher beside me. "That looks so
fun," he said, his eyes tracking the ball, never leaving the field.

But he had talked with the coach at Chicago. James's sense was
that he was good enough to walk onto the varsity team, but probably not good enough to get off the bench much his freshman year.
Maybe not much his sophomore year either. He had not applied as
a soccer recruit. After he got in, he had asked to see the full practice and game schedule. It showed the team practicing daily, traveling most weekends, missing big chunks of spring break and other

holidays to train. Their opponents were all over the place, nearly all of the games requiring long bus rides if not flights. The season that had just finished included games in Atlanta (versus Emory), in Northfield, Minnesota (St. Olaf), Crawfordsville, Indiana (Wabash), Cleveland, Ohio (Case Western), and Pittsburgh (Carnegie Mellon), among others. Twenty-three games total, plus scrimmages and team dinners and sessions with the trainers and all the other commitments that come with playing a varsity sport. It would be, in other words, a continuation of James's high school career, during which every spare second has been consumed by travel soccer plus the two varsity sports he has played through school, soccer and lacrosse. James says he has talked it through with the Chicago coach, more than once, and he's made his decision: he's had enough.

Nick seems to have seen this coming in a way that I didn't.

"Way to go out on top," he says. They high-five across the table and keep eating.

Afterward, as we clear the dishes, I ask Nick about his muted reaction.

"Soccer has been his whole life," I say. "He's played since he could walk."

"I know. I taught him. But he was always going to stop one day."

This, of course, is true. The irony is that had James leaned the other way and announced he was determined to play, I might have tried to talk him out of it, or at least questioned him carefully about the trade-offs that would entail at the college level. And part of me feels nothing but relief that he won't get injured anymore. I have made many—way too many—trips to the emergency room over the years. He has suffered and come back from a broken shoulder, a stress-fractured spine, pulled hamstrings, jammed fingers, and more split lips and bruises and bloody toes than I can count. High school sports are rough. One bad tackle can end a player's season, or his entire career. I am not a particularly religious person, but sometimes during this last season, I would find myself making the sign of the cross across my chest as the final whistle blew. Whatever the score, it felt like a victory if both James and Alexander came off the field intact, whole, walking not limping.

But in bed that night of the panfried chicken, a slideshow played through my head. *Click*. James, age two, dribbling a tiny ball around our old kitchen. *Click*. Age three, wearing a look of fierce concentration and a T-shirt that hung past his knees, at Coach John's neighborhood soccer playgroup, on Friday afternoons at the park at the top of our hill. *Click*. Age five, his first real team, christened the Dirty Dawgs and coached by Nick and a few other dads in his pre-kindergarten class. The team stuck together for several years, and my nails were reliably chipped and broken during these years, because it was my job every Saturday morning to set up the collapsible Pugg soccer goals, to anchor them in mud that had hardened, under the pounding of thousands of tiny cleats, to the consistency of concrete. While I did this, Nick and James would pace the field, debating offensive strategy for the game. The fact that none of the kids, including James, were skilled enough to pull off the elaborate scoring schemes they cooked up did not dampen their enthusiasm in the slightest. *Click*. Age eight, the nerve-racking first tryouts for travel soccer. *Click*. Age ten, when we moved to Italy on sabbatical and both boys played for a team named Impruneta Tavarnuzze, in the neighboring village, where they learned a few gorgeous soccer moves and a lot of truly offensive Italian swear words. *Click*. Age twelve, middle school tournaments. *Click*. Age fourteen, James pounding the treadmill and swilling protein shakes in preparation for high school varsity tryouts. *Click*. Age seventeen, the debacle that was junior year, the entire season decimated by Covid. *Click*. Age eighteen, the come-from-behind triumph of senior year, the marvelous season that ended with them winning the league and the cup. *Way to go out on top.*

It feels important to note that this was all James, all his initiative. Neither Nick nor I are jocks. We've always encouraged the boys to play any sport they like, or none at all. If I'd had a vote for the animating passion of their childhoods, I might have cast mine for piano or cello. Instead they've asked us to sign them up for lacrosse, and for basketball, and for baseball and golf and horseback riding and Tae Kwon Do. They liked them all. But one reigns supreme. If I were to print these images clicking through my head, spread them across a table, and ask you to study them and identify any common thread, it would not take you long to name the look of authentic joy on James's face. You can't miss it. Shot after shot of him flying down the field, hustling so fast neither foot is touching the ground, his face lit up with purpose. The kid loves soccer.

Now, just like that, he's done.

That night I knock at his bedroom door to kiss him good night. I am thinking about how I hadn't realized, back on that electric night at the state championships, the night James scored the *OMFG* goal that won the game 2–0, that I might be watching him play his last competitive soccer game ever. I am thinking of the thousands of grass-stained uniforms and smelly socks I must have washed over the years. The mountains of turf pellets that I've shaken out of shoes into the hedges outside the back door. The dozens upon dozens of snack duty slots I've signed up for, the ones that dutifully instruct parents to bring baggies of sliced apples and carrot sticks. You learn fast that if you want your kid to speak to you on the drive home, you show up with doughnuts instead.

"Thank you for making me a soccer mom," I tell him. "We are proud of you. Always."

He nods and talks about new activities he's excited to try. He wants to get involved with the Institute of Politics on campus, and to volunteer on a campaign. He mentions neighborhoods I've never heard of that he wants to explore in Chicago.

I search his face as he speaks. There is no angst that I can detect. Whatever internal demons he's wrestled with to make this decision, he appears to have vanquished them.

A few days later, I walk back into James's room for something. I discover him using his fingernails to claw years of old stickers and decals off the wood frame of his bed. They are from clothing brands he used to admire, summer camps he used to attend, sports teams he used to play for. He is literally scraping away his childhood, discarding interests that animated him just a year or two ago. His fingernails look like mine used to, toward the end of the Dirty Dawg season, snaggled and filthy. I glance down. On the floor beside James's bed is a fresh sheet of University of Chicago stickers, ready to apply.

I watch for a moment, then offer to find Windex and a razor blade to help.

It's official.

He's outta here.

WE'RE NEARLY HOME (SECOND ATTEMPT)

I F A MANHATTAN WAS MY FATHER'S DRINK, RUNNING WAS HIS SPORT. My God, he loved to run. Dad would lace up and head out in any weather, for any distance, from circuits around our back yard to the Marine Corps Marathon. But his true love, alongside my mother, was the Peachtree Road Race. The Peachtree is the highlight of the Atlanta running calendar, the city's signature race, transpiring every year on the Fourth of July. My father ran it religiously for close to forty years. And for many of those years, he invited, cajoled, and bribed my baby brother and me to run it too.

Atlanta is hot as hell in July, and the course unfurls, as the name suggests, straight down Peachtree Road, the main artery of the city. Six-point-two sweltering, shade-bereft miles of asphalt, south from Lenox Square until you finally hit the blessed green patch that is the final few hundred yards through Piedmont Park. If you were too old to run, or too young, or pregnant—and these were pretty much the only excuses accepted, though I certainly tried a few others over the years—then your job was to decorate a poster, plant yourself along the course, and cheer on everyone else.

Some context: It wasn't just the Peachtree. C.J. and I were force-marched to more Turkey Trots and Jingle Bell Jogs over the years than I care to recall. One of my earliest clear memories dates from when I was four or five years old, and my parents signed me up for a one-mile Fun Run. I was flying, rounding the final turn and headed toward the home stretch, when I spotted a familiar head bobbing between the bushes alongside the course: Dad, sent by Mom, to make sure I was okay.

When my brother and I hit our teens, all these races were grudgingly shifted from the mandatory to the optional category. But it's fair to say we were *strongly* encouraged to run.

"I'll register all of us, so you have timing chips and numbers. Just in case," Dad would say, the note of hope in his voice unmistakable and, at the time, infuriating.

"I told you, Dad. I'm probably busy," I'd reply, mostly just to be ornery. Before he went to bed, Dad would lay out my race number on the hall carpet outside my bedroom, along with safety pins to secure it to my shirt. When he was in especially crafty form, alongside would be a peanut butter and chocolate Power-Bar—my favorite—and a handwritten note: "I would love to run with you."

Fast-forward to six a.m. The alarm buzzing, me warm under the covers, desperate to stay there. But the guilt—knowing he was awake, knowing he was rustling around the kitchen, brewing coffee for a thermos, wondering if I would join him on the dark drive to the starting line—it was almost always enough to rouse even surly teenaged me out of bed and into my sneakers.

Somewhere along the way, I'll concede that I started to like it. Dad cheered me on at high school track meets, which I never won. He cheered me from the sidelines of the 2000 New York City Marathon, the only marathon I've ever run or ever will. Running was something we could share. It's only now that I realize how, at six feet three, he must have shortened his stride for me. Only now I realize that as he loped along beside a younger me, asking inane questions about things not remotely on my mind . . . that he was trying to communicate, groping for a connection, because he had no idea what *was* on my mind. I get it now that I have teenagers of my own, whose interior lives are hidden from me. I find myself groping around with my own inane questions. Asking, the hope naked in my voice, if maybe later they want to go for a run with me? ("I told you, Mom. I'm probably busy.")

Dad was as stubborn about running as he was about everything else. That life lesson about never giving up? Dad's unofficial motto. The man would not quit. He preached walk breaks for distances longer than 10K, and he would walk one minute for every eight or nine that he ran. He said it was easier on your knees, and easier to persuade yourself to keep going if you knew that a chance to walk and catch your breath was never more than eight minutes away. Mile after mile after mile, my father kept going.

As for the rest of us, he possessed a pure, unshakable conviction that *everyone* was a runner, if only they would give it a try. A thousand weekend mornings in our house must have unfolded something like this:

Dad (cautiously optimistic): Want to head over to the river and do a loop on the Chattahoochee trail?

Mom (sweat averse, has never expressed interest in jogging in her entire life): No, thank you.

Dad: It would be good for you. We could pick up bagels afterward.

Mom: You go ahead.

Dad: It's a beautiful morn—

Mom: *JIM*.

My father, Jim Kelly, was diagnosed with cancer in his late fifties. He fought it for seventeen years. Did I mention the man did not quit? Through radiation and surgeries, through chemo—so many, many sessions of chemo—he tried to keep running.

The first year of the pandemic, Dad was too sick to run the Peachtree Road Race. My brother had turned his ankle, so he was out too. Which struck all of us as fine, because the race had been rendered unrecognizable anyway. Covid had forced organizers to delay it from July 4 to Thanksgiving, and then to shift the whole thing from in person to virtual.

I signed up anyway. They mailed my T-shirt and official number, with instructions to run whenever and wherever I wanted, so long as I submitted my results via the official race app. You feel a little silly pinning a big number on your chest when you're running all by yourself, on a random course of your own devising. But I figured: what the heck. Afterward, I gave my number to Dad and told him maybe the next year we'd be back out there together.

We lost my dad three months later. I ran the day he died and every day the week after. And then I found . . . I couldn't. Just couldn't get myself out of bed and out the door. What was the point? Weeks passed and I tried again. Baby steps. Slow and creaky. An eleven-minute mile felt like a triumph.

When the Peachtree came around again, I balked and procrastinated about signing up. It felt so strange to contemplate the race without him. And the world was still strange as well: the pandemic was not done with us yet, and this time the race was hybrid, meaning you could select to run in person or virtually. I chose the latter. I went through the old rituals, laying out my dorky race number the night before, along with safety pins and a peanut butter and chocolate PowerBar. I felt my father's presence as I did these things, sensed him nodding in approval.

On July 4, I picked a solitary course, winding north from my house on the trails along Rock Creek. It felt good to be out there, good to be alive, to be moving, putting one foot in front of the other. I walked one minute to every nine that I ran. It *is* easier on your knees. At the end I went to upload my results to the official race app and did a double take. I had run a personal best. My fastest 10K ever. That seemed unlikely at the age of fifty, but when I examined the mile splits I saw that while I'd started out at my usual pace, I had gotten faster and faster as I ran, with the final mile the fastest mile of all.

I credit Jim Kelly. He'd been keeping me company. As I ran, I heard his voice, pacing me, leaning down to murmur in my ear: "Looking strong! Want to pick it up a little? You got this, buddy. Just a bit farther. We're nearly home."

✳

MY SONS DID NOT INHERIT THEIR GRANDFATHER'S LOVE OF RUNNING, OR AT LEAST THERE'S NO EVIDENCE YET IN THAT DIRECTION. I've never seen them head out for a spin around the neighborhood just for the hell of it. Perhaps all those mandatory laps during soccer and lacrosse practice have drained any love of running for running's sake right out of them.

James did get my father's height, his broad shoulders, and wavy, dark hair. He got Dad's first name, of course. And he got Dad's giggle. My father was a serious man—an attorney with a practice focused on complex corporate and regulatory issues for healthcare providers, a former Army officer, an usher at our church. But sit him down in front of, say, *Saturday Night Live* reruns, or an old Chevy Chase movie, and he would lose it. Clark Griswold would appear and Dad would start to chuckle and then his shoulders would start to shake. You couldn't help but laugh if you were in the vicinity, which only egged him on, until he was howling, clutching the arms of his chair to keep from falling out, utterly slayed by mirth. James is the same. Watching them watch a movie together, cracking themselves up, was always way more entertaining than whatever was happening on-screen.

Alexander, meanwhile, looks nothing like my father. Trimmer build, pale blue eyes, freckles, and bright red hair—he carries the Scottish genes for that generation. But he also carries his American grandfather's love of nature and the outdoors. My father was born and grew up in the American West, and while Alexander did not, he inherited the instinct toward mountains and dry air and big sky. While James is a city boy to his core, Alexander wanted to learn how to ride a horse, and how to build a rabbit trap with his own hands, and how to shoulder a rifle. He loves animals and he loves to hunt, and like my father, he sees no contradiction there.

If the boys did not inherit Dad's passion for running, they did inherit something that you would swear bypassed my genes entirely: speed.

The summer that James was thirteen and Alexander was eleven, back when I still held enough sway over them to dictate our weekend plans, I signed us up for a family road race. The course was 5K on a flat gravel path along the C&O Canal. It runs west from Georgetown into Maryland, and in July it was swollen with weeds, thick with mosquitoes, and wretched with humidity. It's fair to say that no one else in the family was excited about this initiative, especially early on a Sunday morning. I had to bribe them with the prospect of bagels afterward (total Jim Kelly move).

We were by then well past any question as to whether parent or child would win in an all-out sprint. Both boys had been faster than me for years; they could clobber me in a hundred-yard dash. But they never jogged, and I pounded out a few miles most mornings. Not that it was a competition, but I figured that over a longer distance, endurance and experience might still carry the day over youth. I imagined cheering my family across the line, having finished ahead of them, and as we did a recovery lap and made our way toward brunch, I might share my accumulated wisdom about the importance of stretching beforehand and pacing yourself on the first mile.

James crossed the tape seven minutes and fifty-four seconds ahead of me. I still had nearly a mile left to run when he finished. He came in first in his age group, eighth in the entire field of runners. Alexander, two years younger, was close behind. The photos show my face purple with heat exhaustion and both of them barely flushed and grinning, medals swinging from their necks.

"I did it for Papa," James announced. "Can we get food now?"

I'm not sure if either boy has run a 5K since, unless it was under duress by a coach wielding a stopwatch on the track during pre-season fitness drills. I hold out hope that they might yet grow into a jogging habit, if only for the comfort that a long, slow trot can bring. Running has saved me in dark moments. Years ago, Dad told me that when life seems impossible, you should go for a run and then pour yourself a cup of coffee. You might just begin to glimpse a path forward. As with a lot of things, he was right.

✳

I KNEW THE FIRST ANNIVERSARY OF DAD'S DEATH WOULD BE TOUGH, ESPECIALLY ON MY MOM. I invited her to come up and stay with us for the week, so she wouldn't be on her own in the house where she and Dad had lived for twenty-five years, the same house where he had died. A friend had taught me the beautiful Jewish tradition

of Yahrzeit—observing the anniversary of the death of a loved
one by burning a candle for the entire day. Mom and I picked a
stout one, heavily scented and with a double wick, and I lit it on a
table in the living room, early that morning before heading out for
my run. The whole house smelled like cappuccino all day. Dad, a
lifelong coffee fiend, would have loved it.

The following afternoon, a note arrived from three of the
FONs. They had remembered the anniversary of Dad's death
too, and had chosen to mark it by making a donation to the
Atlanta chapter of a group called GirlTrek. It's a nonprofit that
puts together walking teams and encourages African American
women and girls to form a daily habit of exercise. The idea is
to inspire girls to take literal steps toward healthy living, healthy
communities, and a civil rights–inspired health movement.

"To commemorate your Dad who found power in running,"
read the note from the FONs, "and in honor of the superhuman
woman power that you and your Mom exemplify."

My father would have loved this gesture. He would have
endorsed the idea of supporting an organization like GirlTrek.
Beyond that, he would have appreciated knowing the FONs were
looking out for Mom and me. Dad had known these three women,
had danced with them at my wedding, had cooked them bacon
and eggs for breakfast, when they passed through Georgia and
stayed at our house over the years. He always asked after them,
and as their families and their lives expanded, he asked after their
husbands and children too. "How is Sasha?" he would ask. "How
is Jess? How is Kat?"

My father taught me to be a runner. He taught me to mix a
mean Manhattan. He taught me to keep going, to try my hardest,
to never give up. But it is my female friends who have just taught
me something beautiful: that while we may lose a person we love,
their love is not lost to us. It simply finds its way to us through

different channels. Writing this, I feel the arms of strong women reaching out to encircle my mother and me and hold us tight. And I feel Dad in that circle too, right there with us. My friends are showing me how to take grief, and to sit with it, for as long as you need to—and then to turn it into love.

A few weeks later, an email arrives. "Lock in your Fourth of July plans right now and sign up for the Atlanta Journal-Constitution Peachtree Road Race!" it orders, adding, "You can't miss it."

Well, obviously.

I click immediately to sign up, and to run in person this year, in Atlanta. Enough already with virtual races, with pinning on my dorky race number to jog by myself. I text C.J. to tell him. He writes back right away: he and his wife, Jenn, will run with me. No cajoling or bagel bribe required. This feels right. Running the Peachtree is what the Kellys do on the Fourth of July. Maybe one of these days I'll talk my boys into running too.

It occurs to me that this time, as opposed to the year before, I felt no strangeness or hesitation about registering. Is that because of the passage of a year? Yes, in part, of course. Time does not heal all wounds, but it does lessen their intensity; how else could we humans go on? But it's also because of the realization that the thing that had made me flinch—the idea of running this particular race without my father—is perhaps not a bridge I will ever need to cross.

My father's love keeps finding its way to me through different channels. I see him in my sons. I see him in my brother. I feel him in my friends. And if I need to, if I'm tempted to quit at some point during those six-point-two sweltering, shade-bereft miles of the Peachtree, I'll hear his voice. Strong as it ever was. Pacing me.

"Don't worry," he's saying. "I'm right here with you. You got this, buddy. Almost there. Don't give up. We're nearly home."

WAR

———◦•◦———

ANOTHER DAY, ANOTHER BROADCAST, ANOTHER PHONE CALL.
Once again I am on-air when my phone lights up with an
incoming call, and once again, I see that it is James. Strange. It's a
weekday, a Thursday, and he is supposed to be at school, in class.
Something must be up, but once again I cannot answer: I'm in the
middle of live war coverage. Hours before, Russia had invaded
Ukraine.

"This is live special coverage from NPR News," I have just
intoned. Hundreds of stations coast-to-coast are interrupting their
regular programming to carry this. "I'm Mary Louise Kelly in
Washington. . . ."

I let James's call roll over to voice mail. One minute later, he
calls again. I've got one eye on a live feed of President Biden and
the script that I'm reading, both up on a split-screen in front of
me, and the other eye on the cell phone in my hand, lighting up
with my son's caller ID. I still can't answer, and now I'm worried.

The president is addressing the nation from the White House,
threatening sanctions and announcing new U.S. troop deploy-

ments to Europe. Russia has attacked from three directions, north, east, and south. There's a sense that we have woken up to a changed Europe, that this will be no limited strike but all-out, full-country combat, that things could get very, very bad before they get better. A former chairman of the Joint Chiefs of Staff has just appeared on *Morning Edition* and pronounced that the world order has shifted.

I need to listen closely, to take notes as Biden speaks so that I can sum up the headlines the second he finishes and then flip to a panel of NPR reporters for analysis. Three of them are live on the line, in a holding pattern, waiting for the speech to wrap, which could happen at any moment; we don't know whether the president plans to deliver remarks for two minutes or two hours. On a second big screen in front of me, editors from across the network's Washington, International, and National Desks are generating a rolling stream of commentary in our Slack channel for special coverage. They're fact-checking in real time, suggesting questions I might want to put to their reporters, flagging Biden's most newsworthy quotes for colleagues on Newscast and digital teams. I'm tracking all of it, monitoring the president as he turns to questions from the reporters seated before him in the East Room, and ideally I should be finding a moment to live-tweet the proceedings and direct followers on social media to our national broadcast coverage.

But now, on my phone, a text from James: "I have Covid."

This gets my attention. Their school conducts mandatory Covid tests for students every Wednesday. The results must have just come back.

"Oh no," I text back. "Sorry am in middle of live coverage so could not answer. Love you and it will be ok."

Three minutes later, the president is still talking, and James calls yet again. I picture my son, a little scared and not sure what to do. I also am not sure what to do. But on my desk I have what's known as a "cough button," which temporarily silences my microphone if, say, I need to cough and don't want to subject everyone listening to the experience. I stare at Biden on the screen before me. With every ounce of urgency in my body, I will him to keep talking, to hold the floor for another minute. *Don't you dare stop speaking now.* Then I hit my cough button and take the call.

James reports that he feels fine. His nose is stuffed up, that's it. But he is of course being sent home immediately. He won't be allowed to return to school for at least five days, and then not until he can produce a negative Covid test. I tell him to bring home all his books, to clear everything from his locker. James is processing the implications. He's going to miss class and sports and extra-curricular obligations and weekend parties that he was looking forward to.

"And what happens if my test keeps coming back posit—"

"We'll figure it out," I tell him. "Peach, I need to go."

On my screen, Biden finishes answering a journalist. I have no idea what the question was, no idea what the answer was; the president turns from the podium to exit the room. I release my cough button.

"President Biden speaking live there and taking questions at the White House . . ." I begin, then tick through the key takeaways. "More sanctions on Russia, although not on Vladimir Putin himself," I continue, and if I've missed something crucial while I was on the phone with my son, listeners will have to wait for one of my brilliant colleagues to bring it up. Which they do: White House correspondent Tamara Keith has thoughts on the impact of war on oil markets. National security correspondent Greg Myre weighs in on what it will mean to send more American troops to Europe. And international correspondent Frank Langfitt, who has dialed in from a bomb shelter in Ukraine, is pinging the group chat: "Please ask me a NATO question!"

I'm herding all these cats from my study, on the second floor of our house in Washington. We're still broadcasting from home, because James is not the only one testing positive for Covid. The United States is at what we hope will prove the tail end of the Omicron surge. For now, case numbers are still alarmingly high, and NPR won't let me back into the studio at headquarters. This produces endless complications for workflow, but in moments like these, I'm grateful to be around.

"Sixty," the director calls down the line into my ear, meaning sixty seconds for me to wrap and then we're out. I run down the headlines one more time and preview our upcoming coverage that evening.

"Thirty," comes the voice in my ear, urgent now.

I name-check and thank my colleagues who've been on air with me.

"Thanks for listening," I say at last. "This has been . . . special coverage . . . from NPR News."

And then what we call the deadroll music swells, and the director tells the studio engineer to kill my mic. We're clear. I peel off my headphones and wander downstairs to see if there's any soup in the fridge. I could have sworn I bought some; who's eaten it? I check my watch, ponder whether there's time to dash to the corner shop across the street to pick up a few cans of Campbell's chicken noodle, and decide that yes, there is. I have another interview coming up, and a meeting with my editorial team to mark up a script after that. Then I'll start applying myself to the logistics of how to quarantine a very social, very athletic eighteen-year-old who feels completely fine in his room for the next five days.

✳

THAT MORNING, AS ARTILLERY STRIKES RAINED DOWN ON CITIES ACROSS UKRAINE, AS PEOPLE SHELTERED IN SUBWAY STATIONS AND AIR RAID SIRENS WAILED IN KYIV FOR FIRST TIME SINCE WORLD WAR II . . . I noticed a tweet.

"I can't stop thinking about the Ukrainian family with the Guinea pig that @NPRKelly interviewed," someone has posted. "My heart is breaking."

I haven't been able to stop thinking about Hanna Hopko either. We've swapped a few messages on WhatsApp, but I haven't spoken with her since we sat together in a pizzeria in Kyiv, back at the end of January, back in what now feels like another lifetime.

When she answers her phone on the day of the Russian invasion, Hopko sounds as determined as ever, but she also sounds tired. She tells me she's had to flee her apartment in Kyiv, because she fears she's on Russia's so-called kill list, a list of prominent Ukrainians to be detained and imprisoned, or worse. The United States has sent a letter to the UN, warning about the list and what it portends for how brutal the Russian campaign could become.

KELLY: Is your family safe?

HOPKO: Also my husband is with me. The guinea pig is with us.

KELLY: And your daughter?

HOPKO: Daughter is in western Ukraine. Every . . . almost every hour she's calling me and asking, "Mom, how is Nafanya?"

KELLY: The guinea pig.

HOPKO: "Or is Nafanya . . ." yeah. The guinea pig.

I think about this. It's exactly the scenario Hopko was fretting over, when I'd met her a month ago—that she would buy her daughter the guinea pig she'd been begging for, and then if war came, Hopko would be stuck trying to protect and evacuate both her child and a rodent.

"Are you scared?" I ask.

"No." Her voice becomes fierce. "I'm not scared. . . . It's not time to be scared. Putin has to be scared because he is a little gangster with the heart full of fear."

Six days pass before she writes again. Each of those days brings headlines worse than the last—of Russian forces attacking a Ukrainian kindergarten, an orphanage, a mosque. Newspaper front pages carry images of children clutching teddy bears and boarding trains that will carry them west, toward safety, as their stricken-looking parents wave and prepare to head to the front, toward the fight. It is hard to look at these photos and equally hard to look away. What is happening in Ukraine is unspeakably awful. So when Hopko writes again, her message initially mystifies me: she has sent a link to the website of a butcher in upstate New York.

"Creating Handmade Sausage Since 2021," reads the proud banner.

What on earth?

It takes a minute or two of perusing the website to divine that the butcher, Babs of Buffalo, has named a sausage for Hopko—the H.H. Borscht, incorporating her initials and a nod to the soup that is ubiquitous and beloved in both Ukraine and Russia. The sausage is a beautiful deep red color, flavored with beets, dried cayenne pepper, garlic, and vodka.

"We decided to name this wonderful sausage after Ukrainian activist and former parliament member Hanna Hopko," the website reads. "She is a much braver and courageous person than everyone at this company combined. We first heard about her on an NPR interview."

Below is a link to our interview, and also a photo of Hopko, and an account of the guinea pig situation. "She still has the pet while helping defend her country," reads the website, adding, "All of the profits from this sausage and our Smoked Kovbasa will go towards Ukrainian Refugees."

I choke up. Babs of Buffalo appears to be a small company. How many sausages are we talking here? How big a market can there be for borscht-and-vodka links in Upstate New York? My guess is the campaign will bring in a few hundred, maybe a few thousand dollars in donations. A tiny drop in the bottomless bucket of relief aid that will be needed. But then I consider it from another angle: What price can you put on hope?

"She helped inspire us," the website reads, and I find that I feel the same.

A Ukrainian activist and mom has inspired an American butcher, some five thousand miles away. The butcher has found a small, creative way to stand in solidarity with Ukraine. And Hanna Hopko, watching as bombs hit and buildings collapse and a convoy of Russian tanks bears down on Kyiv, understands that she and her country are not alone.

She wants more from America, of course. She wants the United States and its allies to enforce a no-fly zone, she wants anti-tank missiles and fighter jets and more sanctions, and in the days that follow she is tireless in calling for these things. In early March, Secretary of State Antony Blinken posts a photo of himself with Hopko, the two of them leaning close as she shows him something on her phone. She is with a delegation that has traveled to meet him at Ukraine's border with Poland, and I know without asking that she is using the occasion to press for more help in what she sees as an existential battle for her country's survival.

"Today I met with women of principle and courage," Secretary Blinken tweets. "They are defenders of human rights and I applaud the heroic work they are doing. #UnitedWithUkraine." Five days later, Congress votes to approve $13.6 billion in emergency aid for Ukraine. The money includes billions to help refugees, billions for food and health care for Ukrainians and their neighbors, and billions for weapons and military supplies. Against such sums, the sausage fundraiser feels like . . . small beans. But as Hopko and the guinea pig have demonstrated, the small things can be mightily important.

"Oh Hanna," I write back. "I look forward to trying that sausage with you when all this is done. You are OK? And your daughter? And Nafanya? Thinking of you all, every day."

※

So, HOW WOULD YOU FEEL ABOUT GOING BACK TO UKRAINE?"
    This is one of the newsroom's senior editors asking. By mid-March, NPR is fielding a sizable team on the ground in Ukraine—producers, reporters, photographers, plus security consultants and several local journalists serving as our fixers and interpreters. But the boss needs an anchor on the ground, and the *Morning Edition* team that's been there and doing great work these last several weeks is ready to cycle out. So how about it? Do I want to go back?

The truth is yes. Yes, please. Very much.

There are a few factors at play here. The first is simple: I want to go because it's what I do. It's the job, and I am good at it. In his book *Being Mortal*, the surgeon Atul Gawande accurately describes the joy that flows from being good at your work.

"You become a doctor for what you imagine to be the satisfaction of the work, and that turns out to be the satisfaction of competence," Dr. Gawande writes. "It is a deep satisfaction very

much like the one that a carpenter experiences in restoring a fragile antique chest. . . . It comes partly from being helpful to others.
But it also comes from being technically skilled and able to solve
difficult, intricate problems. Your competence gives you a secure
sense of identity."

This resonates. There are countless things I cannot do. I can't
restore a fragile antique chest. Unlike Dr. Gawande, I can't per-
form surgery on you. Hell, I can't whistle or snap with my right
hand or change a flat tire or speak Spanish or do a cartwheel. But
take a news team to a conflict zone, interview people, write about
it, anchor network coverage, tell the story of a nation in crisis?
This . . . this I know how to do. I am professionally trained to bear
witness. In a moment when people around the world are aching to
help Ukraine, this is something I can contribute.

There's also the fact that I'm already personally invested in this
story. It's not just Hopko I'm swapping messages with, but others we
met there too. People we interviewed, people we worked with. My
former fixer and I are texting regularly, as he wrestles with whether
to stay in Lviv, and also with how to protect his parents, because he
can't convince them to evacuate from eastern Ukraine.

The image from this war that I cannot shake, the one that I keep
seeing when I close my eyes, is of four boys I have never met. I write
"boys," but they are men, if only barely. "18 year old Ukrainian
volunteers off to war in Kyiv," reads the caption from the BBC journalist who has posted it. "Three days training and they will be on
the front line." Eighteen years old. The same age as James. I keep
looking at their faces, the faces of strangers, and seeing my son's face
staring back. It's the details in the photo that gut me, details that
betray how very young and unprepared the four of them are. One is
carrying a purple yoga mat. One wears bright white running shoes,
nothing military grade or waterproof about them. They have big
guns strapped across their chests but no helmets, no body armor.

Three wear cheap-looking kneepads, the plastic kind you buy your kids when they're learning to skateboard.

Headed to the front line? After three days' training? Dressed like this?

I understand that boys have been sent to fight and die since the beginning of time. My heart aches for every one of their mothers; as a mother of teenage boys, I stare at this photo and want to weep. As a journalist, though, I feel something closer to rage. I want to go back to Ukraine, find these soldiers, write about them, and make people pay attention. How are we, the alleged grown-ups of the world, allowing this to happen? How could I, one of those grown-ups, not do everything in my power to make it stop?

A third piece of this puzzle is less noble, and it has to do with something I realized about myself long ago. Namely, how much I love being in the field—how energized I feel, far from my family, working like a dog on a big story, even one as grim as this. It has to do with singularity of purpose. On a typical day in the anchor seat in Washington, I'm leaping from an interview on a spike in the unemployment rate, to interviews about Major League Baseball and the latest Supreme Court ruling on abortion and a hiphop album that just dropped. Sometimes all those conversations unfold within the span of a single hour. We don't call it **All** *Things Considered* for nothing. This keeps you nimble. It also keeps you frazzled. As much as I love considering all the things, it is such sweet relief to step away from the fire hose and lock onto just one story. In the field, the non-work demands on my attention largely melt away too. Back home, I'm still overdue to visit the dentist and the clothes dryer is probably still making that ominous clanking sound, but there's not much I can do about it from Donbas.

It's not that I *like* being separated from my family so much as . . . it frees up so much space. The time that I'm in the field is, strangely, the time when I feel least conflicted. It's the only time when I feel something approaching zero guilt. There's probably some analogy to be drawn between the two roles between which I split my time. Here's a stab at it: A journalist in the field is to all other journalists as the mother of a newborn is to all other mothers. Both represent the purest, most intense expression of the role. By which I mean, you hardly sleep. Distractions fall away. Your purpose on this earth is distilled to a single, shining mission.

Get the story.

Keep the kid alive.

The rest is gravy. The rest, for now, can wait.

I F YOU'RE THINKING THAT ALL OF THIS ADDS UP TO A SLAM-DUNK CASE FOR SAYING YES TO MY BOSS, PULLING DOWN A SUITCASE, AND STARTING TO PACK, YOU WOULD BE CORRECT. Except . . . except that set against all of the above reasons to go back to Ukraine is one that casts a powerful no vote.

It's that clock again.

These days I count the weeks. Before, it was months. Soon it will be days.

The clock is ticking faster as James's time at home runs out. As I type, fewer than two months remain until he graduates from high school. NPR is looking for a commitment of at least two weeks. The last NPR anchor to go was away from home for more than a month. War zones are unpredictable. You can't promise you'll make it out on a particular date; you can't promise anything at all other than that you'll do your very best to stay safe and come home when you can. If I say yes to this assignment, I will miss a significant portion of what's left of James's senior year.

When the job and the kids collide, the kids come first.

I call my boss and tell her that I need to sit this one out.

CURVEBALL

SPRING ROLLS IN AND ROLLS OUT AND LEAVES ME PIERCED WITH BOTH GRATITUDE AND SORROW.

On the gratitude side, in no particular order:

Kat comes to visit for Easter. She drives down from Boston, bringing her daughter, Eliza, and also her son, Will. He and James hold court at our Easter dinner table, telling story after story about summer sleepaway camp, how the whole cabin went feral, how much trouble they got in, how close they came to being sent home.

"Remember when we got punished and we had to carry all the canoes with the wasp nests?"

"Remember having to sleep in the art studio because our cabin had bedbugs?"

"Remember the counselor who was always stoned?"

I look at Kat. "We paid how much money for this experience?"

"First I'm hearing of any of this," she replies. "I thought they were sailing all day."

James is laughing too hard to speak, leaving Will to interrupt and finish his thought, exactly as his mother and I have done with each other for the last thirty years.

Meanwhile, Alexander delivers another speech before the whole school, a chapel talk about Ukraine and Russia, drawing parallels to the biblical account of David and Goliath. His focus is on never giving up. He cites some of my recent reporting from the region, quoting a former soldier I met and interviewed in Tbilisi. This means more than he knows, for him to cite my work. Alexander asks me to listen and give feedback as he practices, and he is excellent, so much more eloquent and self-assured than just a few months ago.

On the athletic fields, spring brings lacrosse season. Both boys play midfield, and they work hard at it, though neither is as invested or as good as they are at soccer. Which is, actually, wonderful. Less pressure. It's possible to remember that the point of school sports should be to have fun, to toss a ball back and forth with friends, to stomp around a field as chilly afternoons grow longer and warmer.

Outside our family, I follow and notch other victories.

Hanna Hopko's daughter and Nafanya, the guinea pig, are safe, and the family decides to adopt a puppy next, a sweet-looking Siberian husky whose mother was evacuated from eastern Ukraine.

Marie Yovanovitch publishes her memoir and goes on a book tour. I interview her—the first time I've actually spoken to her—and we have a rich conversation about how she was ousted as ambassador to Ukraine, her decision to testify about the experience, and what she learned about leadership and survival.

Brooke Shields comes on *All Things Considered*. She's on a mission to celebrate her body and her looks as she ages, and to encourage other women over fifty to do the same. She is charming and candid discussing her battles with self-doubt; it is touching to glimpse that even Brooke Shields misses what she once had.

"I don't look like I did in my twenties," she tells me. "My skin is looser. My butt's lower, my love handles and—you know what I mean?"

Yep.

But she also describes how proud she is to star in a new Jordache jeans campaign, how she finally owns her sex appeal for the first time, at the age of fifty-six, more than four decades after a teenaged Brooke achieved instant icon status with the declaration that nothing came between her and her Calvins.

"There's no shame in being older and getting older," she says, adding, "Why can't I be sexy at this age?"

I resist, barely, the urge to wolf-whistle.

In Washington, Ketanji Brown Jackson is nominated to the U.S. Supreme Court, where she will be the first Black female justice. She went to college with me. She and her roommates were one year ahead of me. We must have crossed paths in the dining halls and libraries. That was thirty years ago, and yet somehow it still feels both impossible and exciting that our generation is ready to lead the country. Jackson is so manifestly qualified that her confirmation is never in real doubt. And at her confirmation hearings, she talks about how she didn't always "get the balance right" when juggling motherhood and her job.

"There are lots of responsibilities in the world and . . . you don't have to be a perfect mom," she testifies. "But if you do your best and you love your children . . . things will turn out okay." A photographer captures her teenage daughter, sitting in the row behind her mom, listening and beaming with pride. Love is all over her face. *Oh honey*, I want to say to Judge-about-to-be-Justice Jackson. *You sure as hell got something right.*

But spring also brings a parade of less welcome developments.

Our longtime housekeeper retires and moves away. She's been with us since the boys were babies. She pushed them in their stroller, she helped me fold their onesies. We give her a card and homemade banana bread and a farewell bonus and big hugs. I know I should feel only thankfulness for the many years she has taken care of our family, and I do. But I also feel the loss of a beloved, benevolent presence in our home. I miss her.

Mary Louise Klucky dies. "I have been struggling with this news and have not wanted to tell you," the owner of my namesake chicken writes from Kansas City. They bury her under a poplar tree in the backyard. "Do not have chickens if your heart is tender," the owner adds, with a sad-faced emoji, and I realize I have my answer to whether this chicken was being kept for her eggs or for her meat.

Meanwhile, the war in Ukraine shifts into a slow-motion grind of suffering and devastation. Satellite images reveal that bodies of dead civilians lay in the streets for weeks in Bucha, a suburb of Kyiv. Some had their hands bound, some had bullet holes in their heads. Zelenskyy levels charges of genocide and says Putin is now training his sights on Donbas, preparing for a great battle in Ukraine's far east.

In Atlanta, my mother falls and fractures her pelvis in three places. She is rushed to the hospital, where she remains for two weeks and six days. Then we arrange to have her moved by ambulance to a rehab facility, where she will have around-the-clock nursing care. She has to relearn to walk. To tie her shoes. C.J. and I email paperwork back and forth to each other, trying to figure out her Medicare benefits, and which of us should serve as her legal representative ("to act on behalf of an incompetent or incapacitated resident").

Unspoken but hanging is the question of when or how Mom

can go home. She loves her house; she feels my father's presence there; his closet remains untouched. His favorite hiking boots, ancient and scuffed, still sit where he kicked them off in the laundry room. Their house is full of windows and light. Moonflower vines grow up the railing on the back porch, and when dusk falls on a warm night you can watch the white blossoms popping open, one by one. But the house is also a nightmare of stairs; there are three bedrooms, not one of them on the same floor as the kitchen, and the garage for her car juts off yet another floor. How is this going to work?

On the phone, Mom resolutely refuses to complain. But she cries, a lot.

"Old age is not fun," she sniffles, and I can't find grounds to disagree.

And then, one day, Nick announces that he wants to separate. Things have been difficult for a long time, and we both bear blame for this, and yet the words strike me like a whip.

This year will mark twenty-eight years since our first kiss.

This year will mark twenty-six years since he dropped to one knee, on a bridge in Paris, and held out a ring.

This year will mark our twenty-fifth wedding anniversary.

It was a formal wedding, presided over by a garrulous Catholic priest. Ten groomsmen for Nick. Ten bridesmaids and flower girls for me, garlands of tiny lilies woven in their hair. Nick and his brothers in black tie and newly stitched kilts of Cameron tartan, me in a delicate ivory dress and a veil of French lace that swept the aisle behind me. Dad walked me down that aisle. Nick's father pressed a note into my hands: *Love him as we do, we will love you as he does.*

Now Nick comes bearing a proposal of a different sort: he wants us to take turns living at home, so the boys are not disrupted.

Not disrupted?

Not . . . disrupted?

Teenage boys can be oblivious, but I struggle to imagine what could be more disruptive to James and Alexander than their parents splitting up.

This is not a book about my marriage. That's a story for a different day, a different book entirely. Suffice it to say the air in the house changes. I wander through the rooms, feeling unmoored. In my belly, a tendril of dread uncoils. I sense that everything—everything as I know it—is about to change.

DARKNESS AND LIGHT

———◦⊪◦———

W HEN YOU ARE GOING THROUGH HELL, KEEP GOING.
The words of Winston Churchill, allegedly, though I
can find no reliable record that he ever actually said them. No
matter. They give me courage. I whisper them to myself every
morning as I lie in bed and work to find the will to get up, to face
another day.

Keep going. Keep going.

On good mornings, what follows is this: I lace up my sneakers
and head outside to run past Winston himself. My default route,
the one I take when I want to trot on autopilot, takes me down
a long, gently sloping hill and past the front gates of the British
ambassador's residence here in Washington. Out front, cast in
bronze and leaning lightly on a walking stick, stands the former
prime minister. One of his feet rests on American soil and the
other on the grounds of the British Embassy, a nod both to his
stature as stalwart ally to America and to his U.S. ancestry
(Winston's father was British, but his mother was American. And
yes, I know it's very American of me, but he's in my head so often,

and so often when I am still in my pajamas, that it feels we should be on a first-name basis.) A fat cigar burns in his left hand. His right is raised to flash the trademark "V for Victory" sign.

From across the street, in front of the South African Embassy, a larger-than-life statue of Nelson Mandela answers. His arm is raised in a fist of power salute. "Freedom Fighter, Political Prisoner, Statesman," reads the inscription on the pedestal beneath his feet.

I nod at them as I jog past, thinking: *How did you do it? From where did you summon the courage? Can I borrow a dollop of strength from either of you?* Then I pick up the pace and resolve to pull myself together; if these two could get through everything life threw at them, I can get through the day.

"Never give in, never give in, never, never, never, never." Words that Winston Churchill verifiably did say, on October 29, 1941, in a speech to the students of Harrow School, his alma mater. I channel these words too, as I fight for my marriage, as the silence in our home hardens. Winston, mind you, was speaking to inspire a nation. World War II was raging. London had just survived the Blitz, during which the German Luftwaffe bombed for fifty-seven straight nights. I feel presumptuous harnessing his rhetoric in the face of my private, relatively low-stakes (in the grand scheme of things) turmoil. No bombs are falling at our home. No air raid sirens howl. This spring, the only blitz we are living through is a sudden blitz of parties. High school graduation season hits like a tsunami. Invitations arrive daily for seniors and their parents, to ceremonies and celebrations for which I require a wardrobe of what Winston might have referred to as frocks. I have to dig deep in my emerging-from-the-pandemic closet to find anything suitably pretty, and as for high heels and non-elasticized waists, I fear we may have parted ways for good.

One of these parties unfolds at our house. A record number of boys from James's class are headed to the University of Chicago.

Some of them I know well, but some I've never met, so we invite the whole lot and their parents over for brunch. We serve platters of chicken skewers and crab cakes and raw veggies, which everyone ignores. Another mom brings dessert, cupcakes topped with a tiny sugar diploma rolled up and tied with red ribbon. James stands and offers a toast to his classmates: "We're going to be friends forever. You guys are always welcome in my dorm room. You can crash there anytime." I grin and am tempted to inject, sotto voce, "Have you SEEN the state of his bedroom upstairs? The litter of dirty socks and dirty plates? Trust me, keep your distance." Instead I keep my mouth shut and top up the parents' wineglasses. We chatter about summer plans. The boys debate how to game the freshman housing lottery, the merits of singles versus doubles. It is such a nice day, both kids and parents bursting with pride and excitement for what lies ahead.

One graduation ritual that I have a feeling will stay with me a long time is one that I did not witness. The seniors finish school a week before everyone else, and Alexander tells me that on their last full day of classes, they formed a ring around the traffic circle in front of the Upper School entrance. All of the other grades and the full faculty lined up and, one by one, shook each senior's hand, working their way slowly around the whole class.

The next morning, I ask James about it.

"That sounds like a beautiful tradition. What did everyone say as they shook your hand?"

"Oh, you know. 'Good luck.' And 'Congratulations.'"

"That must have felt great."

James swallows and shakes his head, no. "Afterwards everyone went inside and it was only us left. Only the seniors. And we . . . everybody just started crying."

"Why?"

"Because . . . ." There's a catch in his voice. "Because it's over."

✳

B<small>UT THE NEXT DAY IS</small> B<small>EACH</small> D<small>AY, WHICH DOES NOT INVOLVE</small> <small>AN ACTUAL BEACH BUT DOES FEATURE THE SENIORS SPRINTING</small> <small>ACROSS GRASS IN SWIMSUITS, ENGAGED IN AN EPIC GAME OF</small> W<small>IFFLE</small> <small>BALL.</small> Sleepovers follow, and road trips and barbecues. One girl at another school ups the ante by renting a mechanical bull for her graduation party. And then—the pinnacle, toward the end—comes prom, which James seems to look forward to with uncomplicated anticipation, none of the angst that I recall from my own high school dance days.

Perhaps this is the difference between teenaged boys and teenaged girls. Or perhaps there is actually all kinds of behind-the-scenes drama, and James just isn't sharing it with me. Or—most likely scenario?—they're all just too damn happy that it's happening at all, after Covid canceled prom last year, and the year before.

Dinner is served at the dance. Faculty chaperones patrol for hip flasks or anyone with vodka on their breath. James wears a rented tuxedo. The young women wear brightly colored strapless micro-dresses that consist of approximately one square foot of fabric.

Too short to be called frocks? I can hear Winston sniffing.

Easy, now, I would answer. *Remember what it was to be that young? To have legs a mile long that never tired?*

The dresses are hot pink and mint green and lemon yellow. They are gorgeous. They are perfect. The girls look lit up from within. They look—there is no other word for it—enchanting.

Parents are invited to many of the events and parties. Nick and I go together. Sometimes we speak on the drive home. Sometimes not.

✳

T HE DISSONANCE.

The juxtaposition.

The impossible contrast, between the joy of watching James and his friends out together, celebrating their last days of high school, and the loneliness that awaits at home.

I begin to understand that when a marriage dies, you grieve it as you would a person. There is motion. There are stages. Denial, rage, sadness, hope, repeat. I keep the tumult at bay all day, while I work, but it finds me in the evenings. I set the kitchen table for dinner, four places, four forks, four napkins, four glasses. For how much longer?

I meditate on what it means in a marriage to never give in, to never give up. The vows that Nick and I swore before friends and family were unambiguous: *for better, for worse, for richer, for poorer, in sickness and in health, . . . until death do us part.*

We are not dead.

We are very much alive.

I find and study a passage that I hand-copied into my journal, from Jonathan Safran Foer's 2016 novel, *Here I Am.* It reads, "Only one thing can keep something close over time: holding it there. Grappling with it. Wrestling it to the ground, as Jacob did with the angel, and refusing to let go. What we don't wrestle we let go of. Love isn't the absence of struggle. Love *is* struggle."

So I struggle. I wrestle. I refuse to let go.

Why should things be easy when they can be difficult?

Weeks pass.

The unmoored feeling persists. Some days, standing in our front hall and looking up the stairs toward the bedrooms, I feel something like vertigo. Did that wall just sway? And there, out of the corner of my eye, did I spy the hardwood floor wobble and tilt? I press a hand to my temples and remind myself, sternly, that the walls and the floor are solid. The house is *fine.* It is my relations with its occupants that are off-balance. It is supposed to be the four of us against the world. I have tethered my identity to the people in these rooms, have defined myself in relation to them for most of my adult life.

I am a wife. I am a mother.

Who was I, before these things? Who did I use to be?

I HAVE KEPT A JOURNAL, ON AND OFF, SINCE I WAS A CHILD. I still have all my journals, stacked in a deep drawer in my bedroom. The original volume is a tiny green spiral notebook that begins early in 1979, when I would have been seven. The entries are neatly printed—I had not yet learned cursive—in No. 2 pencil. "My Best Friends in second grade are . . ." reads the first page, and five names follow, one of them a friend from Atlanta with whom I am still in touch. Volumes follow that move through my ballerina phase, my horse phase, then into high school and college. As an adult, whole years pass when I appear not to have written at all. The early years of my marriage are notable for this; I had found a soul mate, and we had no secrets, and who needs to vent to a journal when you're sharing every thought that flits through your mind with another human?

I met Nick when I was twenty-three. The diary I pull out now is the last before he appeared on the scene. It is dusty pink and battered and spans the period from late college through graduation through moving back to Georgia, back into my parents' house, back into my childhood bedroom, and beginning my first real job, as a summer intern and then a full-time political reporter at the *Atlanta Journal-Constitution*.

I am surprised to see how many of the entries are in French, or flipping between English and French, back and forth across paragraphs and sometimes within a single sentence. I had just earned an honors degree in French literature. I spent my college summers in France, either doing research in the great libraries or working for peanuts, just to be there. For years, I was reading and writing and speaking French constantly. I had forgotten.

As for content, the pages explore whether I was dating the right guy (answer: nope), whether I should go to grad school (yep), whether I could lose seven pounds by Saturday night (seems unlikely, but good luck).

I pause on an entry dated February 25, 1994. I also recorded the time: 3:38 a.m. Why was I awake at 3:38 a.m.? This is not clear. "This has been such an odd week," it begins. "I have been depressed, moping, teary-eyed and tense . . . so I came crawling into my bed, gearing up to sob myself to sleep." Why? What was troubling me? Again, not clear.

I do the math. I would have been twenty-two, four years older than James is now. Clearly, I had not outgrown a teenaged proclivity toward melodrama. For some perverse reason, it cheers me up now to see how very miserable I was, back when I did not in fact have any real problems to be miserable about. I was living in a nice house, I was healthy, I had great friends, I was gainfully employed at a job I liked. It's tempting to roll my eyes at the moping young woman who penned this entry. The problem is, all those things hold equally true today. Perennial failure to lose seven pounds aside, life has not handed me challenges I cannot manage. I recognize that I am, then and now, so lucky.

My fifty-one-year-old self vows . . . to lighten up. To try to take things less seriously, to allow myself to laugh more—really laugh, leaning close to a friend, falling together in a fit of the giggles. Even with everything going on. *Especially* with everything going on. So much of life really does depend on what we choose to see.

My journal entry shifts gears, once I've gotten my angst off my chest and onto the page, turning to a reporting dilemma that was nagging at me. I was by then assigned to cover the DeKalb County Board of Commissioners, based out of the paper's Decatur bureau. A key person I needed to interview wasn't returning my calls, and I couldn't figure out how to move the story forward without him. "Need to talk this through with my editor on Monday," I conclude, and fifty-one-year-old me nods approvingly. Yes, that's exactly what you need to do. A good editor can help whack a path through all kinds of journalistic thickets and dead ends.

It hits me: My voice on these pages is recognizable. I know this girl. My now rusty French aside, she sounds just like me. I could have written the passage about tearing my hair out because a source is neglecting to return my calls a hundred times; I could have written it this morning. This girl—not yet a wife, not yet a mother—is already me. She is scared and confused and determined and she is trying her best. I'm rooting for her. This girl is going to be okay.

I closed out the entry by copying four quotations from Rilke; I was prone to quoting him copiously in those years. The last is an excerpt from a longer poem about grief and finding ways to push through it. The poem is beautiful. But looking back, all these years later, the words that hit home are not in fact by Rilke but by Robert Bly, Rilke's translator from the German, who has jotted his own commentary alongside the original work. The line that I copied into my journal, alone and lonely in my childhood bedroom, sometime after 3:38 a.m., on February 25, 1994, was this:

The pain is the cracking of the walls as the room grows.

Yes. Yes, it is. What a lovely way to think about it.

TWO WALKS

———◆———

YOU DON'T ALWAYS KNOW WHEN SOMETHING PRECIOUS IS HAP-
PENING FOR THE LAST TIME.

For example: the last time your about-to-be-taller-than-you, about-to-be-teenager crawls onto your lap for a cuddle. A few years earlier, the last time that same child calls you "Mommy," before a friend teases him, and he is embarrassed, and from there on out, you're "Mom." And of course that heartbreaker we already discussed, the last time this child begs for a bedtime superhero story, because the next night he's shooing you from the room—"And can you close the door behind you?"—so he can read by himself.

Also: the last time you will wake up beside your husband of twenty-five years, having dreamed on pillows side by side. Or: the last time he reaches for your hand, as the two of you stroll a rainy sidewalk, lost in a private conversation, in a world the two of you have built. There will come a last time, but you don't know it in the moment, you can't, not until it's weeks or months or even years in the rearview mirror.

With my father, though. With my father, I think I knew.

He wanted to go for a walk. He had fought cancer for many years but now it had metastasized. The tumors were everywhere. They grew up between his ribs, pressing on his lungs, cracking the bones apart from the inside. You could look at him and see that everything hurt. Anyone else would have retreated to bed and stayed there. But Dad, being Dad, wanted to walk. It would be the last time I ever went for a walk with him, and I think I knew it.

It was December. Christmas. The days as short as they can get. Nick and the boys and I had flown down from DC for the week, and the whole family had rented a cabin in the woods, on a pond in north Georgia. There was a basic kitchen, and a huge fireplace that smoked and spat and required constant tending. My mother baked her famous gingerbread boys, spiked with molasses and brown sugar, and dotted with raisin buttons and eyes. These cookies are my father's favorite. He ate one. It came back up. He kept trying.

Outside, a dirt road led from the cabin, skirted the pond, and disappeared into the pines. This was hunting country, with deer and quail seasons under way, and at dawn the woods rang with the sound of gunfire. By afternoon, though, the air was still.

"Want to go for a walk?" Dad asked.

"Stay with him," my mother whispered to me.

Nick and the boys and I pulled on our boots.

My husband and sons fell into conversation and strode ahead. Dad and I took it slower. We had not gone far before he fell. One moment he was shuffling forward and the next he was not. He stumbled and sank onto the side of the road. He lay there for a bit, panting, before he would allow me to help him up. I felt anger, wanted to reach into his chest and snatch the tumors out, stab them, fling them into the pond to drown, *bastards*. We walked a bit more. Nick and the boys pulled farther ahead until they rounded a bend and we could no longer see them. Dad stumbled again.

Went down again. Longer on the ground this time. He got up. Shuffled forward.

When you're going through hell, keep going.

All around us pine trees and the rustle of a breeze and the whiff of chimney smoke. The light must have been that thin, pale, wintry light, but in my memory, it pulsed strong and golden. I hoped Mom was not watching from the windows. Hoped the boys would not turn around while their grandfather was on the ground. For weeks now, C.J. and I had been trying to tell him: *Dad, it's time to rest. We've got this. We'll take care of Mom. Promise. You can stop fighting now.* He shook us off, ignored us.

"He won't listen," I muttered to my brother. "He just talks over me. He can't do it. We might as well be telling him to stop breathing." And then I realized, with a pang, that that *was* essentially what we were telling him.

As we walked, Dad talked, offering advice, telling me things he thought I needed to know. "Family always comes first," he said. "You need to make the time. You need to take care of the boys. They are such good boys. You need to take care of Nick."

I nodded. The love of a parent runs so deep. The instinct to teach and keep watch over our children is unending. I wrote before, back in the chapter about life lessons and Pompeo, about how you try as a parent to pass on your values, and that you never know what your kids are taking in. Are they listening when you preach about the importance of kindness? When you tell them for the thousandth time how fortunate they are, and that yes, they really do have to write that thank-you note?

Dad, I was listening. I remember it all.

From the pine straw, where he lies sprawled on the side of a dirt road in Georgia, my father looks up at me. His face is gray with pain but his eyes are hopeful.

"Do you think the boys would like to learn more carpentry?"

he asks. "I've got some wood in the garage at home. It's important to know how to use power tools."

He begins to describe, in some detail, the specific power tools on which he wants to instruct James and Alexander.

Oh my God, I think. *Huguenots*, I think.

Dad was seventy-four years old. I was forty-nine. He died seven weeks later. I took his hammers from his workbench in Atlanta and brought them home with me. They are wooden and heavy, old school, and the handles are worn smooth from his hand.

"It's important to know how to use power tools," my father said, and what he meant was *I love you I love you I love you.*

WASHINGTON NATIONAL CATHEDRAL SITS ON A HILL. The towers are neo-Gothic and so tall that on an overcast day they disappear into the clouds. Woodrow Wilson is interred here. So is Helen Keller. The cathedral boasts flying buttresses and ribbed vaulting and a 10,647-pipe great organ that was installed in 1938. It boasts 112 gargoyles. It boasts 215 stained glass windows.

And today, lined up in alphabetical order on the wide limestone steps in front, it boasts seventy-nine nervous boys about to graduate from high school.

James and his classmates have been commanded to turn out in navy blue blazers, white shirts, and white pants. Who decided white pants and teenage boys were a good combo? They have rehearsed where to stand and when, who's in charge of which readings. Their high school graduation is in such a grandiose setting because their school is here. It's one of three schools situated on what's known as the Cathedral Close: the school my boys attend, a girls' school, and a co-ed school for younger kids that both James and Alexander attended through third grade. Proximity to the cathedral can present the odd logistical challenge. This academic year alone, school has been delayed or canceled to accommodate the funerals of Colin Powell, Bob Dole, and Madeleine Albright. The security details and press pools that trail the foreign heads of state, U.S. presidents, senators, and other VIPs who come to pay their respects make it impossible for anyone else to move around. Roads are closed. Secret Service trucks and TV news vans take over the boys' parking spots, power cables snaking across the asphalt.

But today, it's just us.

Moms are passing around preemptive tissues and wondering aloud whether even waterproof mascara will stand up to the torrent of tears that are about to flow. Parents of seniors have been allocated prime seats near the front. Nick and I perch close together, shoulders brushing. Things feel easy between us today. Maybe this means something or maybe it doesn't. Maybe it's okay just to sit companionably, to take pride together in a long partnership that has raised two wonderful boys, that has achieved what we set out to do.

The service opens with a Gaelic blessing, sung by the combined choirs of our school and the boys' sister school.

Deep peace of the running wave to you
Deep peace of the flowing air to you
Deep peace of the quiet earth to you
Deep peace of the shining stars to you
Deep peace of the gentle night to you
Moon and stars pour their healing light on you . . .

The American flag comes down the aisle. Then the school banner. Two by two, the seniors process in. The faculty processes behind them. I had known the Upper School teachers would be here, but I had not expected the entire Lower School to show up as well. The boys' beloved fifth-grade teacher passes me. The Spanish teacher who first drilled them on conjugating *ser* and *estar*. Their first science teacher, known for ambitious lab experiments and for sporting bow ties and crazy pants. It's like watching a parade of parent-teacher conferences over the years whizzing past; I see the faces and remember long-ago problem sets and field trips, group projects that somehow always involved large pizza orders to feed large numbers of boys in our kitchen, and incoming texts wondering whether Nick or I might swing by the hardware store on our way home from work, to pick up a glue gun and paint thinner.

I scan the faces, unsuccessfully, for James's AP statistics teacher this year. He emailed just the night before, subject line: "I need your textbook." A quick scan down the email thread reveals that he has written to James four times over recent days, inquiring with increasing urgency as to when James plans to return his textbook for the course. My son appears to have ignored these notes. So the teacher has escalated, copying Nick and me on his final, beseeching appeal. The result is that I am now at graduation, in my cute outfit with my cute handbag, schlepping a dog-eared, heavily high-lighted copy of that cherished 880-page tome *Introduction to Statistics and Data Analysis* (3rd edition). This is so typically James.

"Mom, could you just, like, bring it in a bag or something?" he had asked, when I set the book at his place at the table that morning.

"Or *you* could just, like, bring it in a bag or something," I reply.

"I would lose it," he says, and we grin at each other, at the unassailable truth of this observation.

To my surprise, the only time that I get misty-eyed during the ceremony is when I spot one of the boys' English teachers. Mr. Schultz assigned them George Orwell and Margaret Atwood; he taught them Shakespeare, *Romeo and Juliet*. He doubles as the varsity soccer coach. He likes to joke that James is responsible for quite a few of the gray hairs on his head. I like to think Alexander will add a few more strands to the tally by the time he graduates. Both of my sons adore Mr. Schultz.

The 10,647 pipes of the great organ are deafening as he passes me, in his academic gown, on his way up the aisle toward the altar and the faculty seats. There's no chance to speak. But I catch his eye.

Thank you, I mouth.

He nods. *You are so welcome.*

I don't know why that was the moment that got me, the one that made me choke up. I think it had to do with how it really does take a village, with the sheer number of people packed into this space today who have helped and disciplined and cared for my children.

I am so, so grateful.

NICK IS AN EXCELLENT PHOTOGRAPHER. He snaps terrific pictures of all the pageantry and proceedings. But my hands-down favorite is one that he catches of James, as he strides past us on his way in. He is wearing my father's necktie, one of several that he chose from Dad's closet in Atlanta. And he is looking not at Nick's camera but slightly to its left. I zoom in. He is looking at me. Straight at me. He has the sweetest look on his face. A small, almost shy smile. It is the look he used to give me when he was a little boy and he wanted to show me something he had built, something that he was really proud of.

Nick's camera has captured something that is hard to capture in words, because it exists at a level at which there is no need for words. I have loved this boy since the day he was born. Our bond has changed and stretched and been tested, sometimes sorely tested, over eighteen years. But perhaps the pain was the cracking of the walls as the room grew. Because there it is, clear as day on my son's face: the simple, sweet love between a boy and his mama.

✳

IN THE OPENING PAGES OF THIS BOOK, I PROPOSED AN EXERCISE. It was to think of my life as a play in—so far—three acts. The curtain was about to open on Act III.

I posed a couple of questions: What now? What next?

I did not imagine when I began writing this, a year or so ago, that these would be quite such open questions.

I think about my work. My NPR contract is up for renewal soon. Should I stay? It is possible to stay somewhere too long. I wonder when it will be time to push outside my comfort zone, to choose a new adventure, to try something entirely different. But I am happy. I like my job. I am good at it. I know how rare that is, to have found work that feels deeply satisfying, work that I look forward to on a Monday morning.

I decide to go back to Ukraine.

I think about where I want to live, in another two years when it is Alexander's turn to process through this cathedral, when there are no more children in the house, nothing requiring me to stay in Washington.

I think about who I want to be living *with*.

I love my husband. I do not know where things between Nick and me will land. I do know that life is made up of big decisions but small rituals, like who makes your coffee in the morning and whether, when you come downstairs to drink it, they are happy to see you.

The day before graduation, the headmaster had given a talk about rituals. He told the assembled seniors and their families to find comfort in them, to use them to help navigate this time of transition and emotion and farewells.

"We are filled with sadness to see you go," the headmaster tells the seniors. "But how lucky we are to have had you here, to have something that makes it so hard to say goodbye."

✳

THERE IS A TRADITION ON THE FIRST DAY OF SCHOOL EVERY YEAR. The very youngest boys process into the cathedral, flanked on each side by a senior. The older boys are showing them how it's done, welcoming them to the rituals and to their ranks. The school spans nine years, from fourth through twelfth grades. It is difficult to wrap your mind around how much growth happens in these years, until you see the start and the finish lines side by side. The seniors have a couple of feet and, in some cases, a couple hundred pounds on the little guys. They have become men. If you're the parent of a fourth grader, you marvel at the hulking upperclassmen and contemplate just how much you're going to need to shell out on food in the coming years to underwrite this transformation. If you're the parent of a senior, you marvel at how tiny they were, not so very long ago.

I always think of a fresco in one of my favorite churches in Florence. Masaccio painted it around 1424 on the wall of Santa Maria Novella. It shows the Holy Trinity: Christ on the cross, God the Father, and the Holy Spirit. Beneath them lies a skeleton in a tomb, and an inscription, in Italian: "What you are I once was; What I am, you will be." A reminder that our time is short. A reminder that it goes so fast.

Today, after the diplomas are conferred, after the last hymn is sung, the boys line up one final time, to reverse their steps and process out. Out of the cathedral, out of high school, out of childhood, out through the massive front doors and on to the reception that awaits outside.

They begin at a stately pace. But halfway down the aisle, the boys at the front break rank. Some signal, imperceptible to the rest of us, is transmitted from senior to senior, back down the line, and they begin to jog and then to run. Seventy-nine boys-turned-men galloping down the main aisle of the National Cathedral.

Outside they are whooping, singing, arms slung around each other's shoulders, jumping up and down in a pack, and they will never again be so young and so invincible. Cigars are lit. Winston would approve. The bells of the cathedral toll. Parents and grandparents and siblings arrange themselves into every possible permutation for photos. Everyone is thirsty, no one has water, minds begin to turn toward dinner plans.

We spot the statistics teacher in the crowd and hand over the 880-page brick of a textbook.

"Am I the very last one to return this?" James asks hopefully.

The teacher scans his list. "Third from last. Still a couple to go." He hands James two stickers as a reward for the return. Stickers? For an eighteen-year-old? I experience another flashback to fourth grade. My son, who is at that moment smoking a celebratory cigar, thanks him politely and wishes him a good summer.

A T THE VERY END, WHEN THE CIGARS ARE SMOKED, THE TIES ARE LOOSENED, ALL THE PHOTOGRAPHS ARE TAKEN, AND THE RECEPTION IS WINDING DOWN, OUR FAMILY DIVIDES INTO CARS TO HEAD HOME. We had arrived in three separate vehicles, to accommodate houseguests. Nick's parents have flown in from Scotland for the festivities; the boys' favorite longtime babysitter has flown in too.

James and Alexander announce they will ride together, just the two of them. James has the car key in his hand and he is limping. He is wearing dress shoes, lace-up fancy Oxfords that he's not used to, and they have rubbed blisters on both his heels. He's been on his feet for hours and he's in agony. He leans against me, unties and kicks off the offending footwear, pecks my cheek, and starts padding across the grass, toward the parking lot, in his socks.

I want to call after him, to remind James there are Band-Aids in the kitchen drawer for his blisters. I want to tell him to phone his grandmother, my mother, on the drive home, to tell her how it went. I want to tell him that while I'll be driving my own car home, my heart will ride in theirs.

My sons walk away, chattering to each other, calling out to friends. They do not look back. There is so much I want to say but I can guarantee that today of all days they are not listening. What I want to say to James and Alexander boils down to this:

I am proud of you.
I love you.
It's important to know how to use power tools.
Never give up.
Never give in.
Keep going, my beautiful boys.
Keep going.

ACKNOWLEDGMENTS

This book is dedicated to my sons, but it would not exist without the women in my life.

Early in the pandemic, like a lot of people, I began to walk. The point was to move but also to look up at the sky and the trees and to breathe, during a time when life felt frightening and broken. Whole chapters of this book were written on these walks, as I allowed my mind to roam and figure out what it was that I was trying to say.

Other days, though, I brought a friend. My girlfriends showed up to walk with me on fine days and also when it was raining sideways. We walked through the thick swamp of a Washington, DC, summer, and when winter came we skidded and slipped and caught each other on patches of black ice. Anne Mitchell, Avery Gardiner, Miriam Mahlow, Tammy Wincup, Sharon Russ, Susan Glasser, Hannah Isles, Jocelyn Dyer, Alison Schafer, and other lovely friends in Washington: thank you for getting me through the pandemic. Thank you for listening. Friends farther afield sent poems and podcasts and recs for TV shows and photos of the sunrise wherever they were. And they checked in, over and over, with the simplest text—*Hey friend, thinking of you, are you ok?* You all walked with me in spirit, and I felt it, and I thank you.

My thanks to the wonderful editors at NPR, including Courtney Dorning and Jolie Myers, who edited much of the journalism referenced in these pages and made it better. Thanks to the lead producers on my *All Things Considered* host teams, who have crisscrossed the world with me and who, with a single, fabulous exception (Hi, Sam Gringlas!) have all been amazing women: Monika Evstatieva, Becky Sullivan, Andrea Hsu, Fatma Tanis, Kat Lonsdorf, and Jonaki Mehta.

Nick and I raised our boys with the help of a small army of babysitters and au pairs over the years. Thank you to all of them, including Menik Lokuhewa, Andressa Borges, Magda Kowalczyk, and most especially to Claudia Schalling, who has become like a sister to me.

Thanks to my editor, Amy Einhorn, and her superlative team at Henry Holt. Amy saw what I was capable of writing, and then she got out of the way and let me write it.

To my literary agent, Victoria Skurnick, who knows when to nudge and when to nag and when to roll into town and buy me brunch. My heartfelt thanks to her and to the whole crew at Levine Greenberg Rostan, for believing in me and in this book at moments when I quavered.

Finally, most importantly, to my sons. Alexander and James, thank you for letting me share these stories. Thank you for putting up with me. Thank you for making me laugh.

Never, ever doubt how fiercely you are loved.

ABOUT THE AUTHOR

Mary Louise Kelly has reported for NPR for two decades and is now cohost of *All Things Considered*. She has also written two novels, *Anonymous Sources* and *The Bullet*, and is the author of articles and essays that have appeared in the *New York Times*, the *Atlantic*, the *Washington Post*, and the *Wall Street Journal*, among other publications.

A Georgia native, Kelly graduated from Harvard University with degrees in government and French language and literature and completed a master's degree in European studies at the University of Cambridge in England. She created and taught a graduate course on national security and journalism at Georgetown University. In the aftermath of the assassination of General Qasem Soleimani, she led a team to Iran that was named a finalist for the 2021 Pulitzer Prize. In addition to her NPR work, Kelly has served as a contributing editor at the *Atlantic*, moderating newsmaker interviews at forums from Aspen to Abu Dhabi.